# Morning in America

POLITICS AND SOCIETY IN TWENTIETH-CENTURY AMERICA

*Series Editors: William Chafe, Gary Gerstle, Linda Gordon, and Julian Zelizer*

*A list of titles in this series appears at the back of the book.*

# Morning in America

How Ronald Reagan Invented the 1980s

## GIL TROY

PRINCETON UNIVERSITY PRESS

PRINCETON AND OXFORD

Library of Congress Cataloging-in-Publication Data

Troy, Gil.
Morning in America : how Ronald Reagan invented
the 1980s / Gil Troy.
p. cm.
Includes bibliographical references (p. ) and index.
ISBN 0-691-09645-7 (cloth : alk. paper)
1. United States—Civilization—1970– 2. United States—
Social conditions—1980– 3. Nineteen eighties. 4. Reagan,
Ronald—Influence. 5. Politics and culture—United States—
History—20th century. 6. United States—Politics and
government—1981–1989.   I. Title.
E169.12.T765 2004
973.927'092–dc22          2004055295

British Library Cataloging-in-Publication Data is available

This book has been composed in Dante
Printed on acid-free paper. ∞
pup.princeton.edu
Printed in the United States of America
1  3  5  7  9  10  8  6  4  2

*To our four children*
Golden doves, harbingers of spring and righteousness,
with the hope that you will grow:

"To learn knowledge and ethics,
  to master subtleties.
  To embrace the moral discipline of wisdom,
  justice and right and goodness."

PROVERBS 1:2–3

# Contents

# Morning in America

# Introduction

## Ronald Reagan's Defining Vision for the 1980s—
and America

There are no easy answers, but there are simple answers.
We must have the courage to do what we know is morally right.
RONALD REAGAN, "THE SPEECH," 1964

Your first point, however, about making them love you,
not just believe you, believe me—I agree with that.
RONALD REAGAN, OCTOBER 16, 1979

One day in 1924, a thirteen-year-old boy joined his parents and older brother for a leisurely Sunday drive roaming the lush Illinois countryside. Trying on eyeglasses his mother had misplaced in the backseat, he discovered that he had lived life thus far in a "haze" filled with "colored blobs that became distinct" when he approached them. Recalling the "miracle" of corrected vision, he would write: "I suddenly saw a glorious, sharply outlined world jump into focus and shouted with delight."

Six decades later, as president of the United States of America, that extremely nearsighted boy had become a contact lens–wearing, famously farsighted leader. On June 12, 1987, standing 4,476 miles away from his boyhood hometown of Dixon, Illinois, speaking to the world from the Berlin Wall's Brandenburg Gate, Ronald Wilson Reagan embraced the "one great and inescapable conclusion" that seemed to emerge after forty years of Communist domination of Eastern Europe. "Freedom leads to prosperity," Reagan declared in his signature dulcet tones that made fans swoon and critics cringe. "Freedom replaces the ancient hatreds among the nations with comity and peace. Freedom is the victor." Offering what sounded then like a pie-in-the-sky challenge or a pie-in-the-sky prayer, President Reagan proclaimed: "General Secretary Gorbachev, if you seek peace, if you seek prosperity for the Soviet Union and Eastern Europe, if you seek liberalization: Come here to this gate! Mr. Gorbachev, open this gate! Mr. Gorbachev, tear down this wall!"

Another seventeen years later, on June 11, 2004, Ronald Reagan's funeral climaxed a week of Lincolnesque commemorations. Contradicting its own editorial line, the *New York Times* front page hailed Reagan for "project[ing] the optimism of [Franklin D.] Roosevelt, the faith in small-town America of Dwight D. Eisenhower and the vigor of John F. Kennedy." The 2004 Democratic nominee, Senator John Kerry, gushed: "He was our oldest president . . . but he made America young again." The Massachusetts Turnpike, a central artery carrying hundreds of thousands of opponents now often caricatured, eighties'-style, as Chardonnay-sipping, NPR-listening, *New York Times*–reading, Reagan-hating yuppie liberals, flashed an electronic sign saying: GOD SPEED PRESIDENT REAGAN. The respect and affection millions expressed, be it in silence, tears, or wistful reminiscences, constituted Ronald Reagan's final gift to the American people. "He brought us all together for one last time, wherever we were," Reagan's speechwriter extraordinaire Peggy Noonan wrote.

In the 1980s Ronald Reagan offered his fellow Americans a perspective, a set of glasses that helped their "glorious sharply outlined world jump into focus." For some, it was a "miracle" that would see America revive, the Soviet Union falter, and the once seemingly unassailable Berlin Wall fall. For others, Reagan's vision represented a national myopia that was immoral, adolescent, and dangerous. But then as now, whether they "shouted in delight" or muttered in frustration, few could deny Reagan's significance—or the importance of the decade he dominated, as his funeral confirmed.

Reagan's vision represented his keystone contribution to the 1980s, a decade of boom times and boom-time values. Perhaps the biggest consumer revolt of the period came in 1985, when the Coca-Cola company unveiled "New Coke," a sweeter, tangier, more Pepsilike version of America's national beverage. Reporters played the grassroots backlash as a modern American Revolution, defending "baseball, hamburgers, Coke," although some critics simply grumbled that New Coke did not mix well with their rum. When Coca-Cola retreated, Senator David Pryor, an Arkansas Democrat, called old Coke's resurrection "a very meaningful moment in the history of America. It shows that some national institutions cannot be changed." This "rebellion" was a quintessential 1980s' story: in the disproportionate reaction to a minor, symbolic problem; in the application of 1960s' grassroots tactics to a decadent, consumer culture issue; in the anger of "Reagan country" mobilized against change; in the sweet strains of nostalgia and patriotism mingling with self-indulgence; in the gap between the simple media story line and the messier realities.

The centrality of a soft drink to the identity of both New Coke and Classic Coke advocates reflected America's epidemic consumerism. New technologies, ideologies, and bureaucracies, along with revolutions in economics, marketing, advertising, and conceptions of leisure, had transformed the cautious American customer, once wary of chain stores, into the 1980s' sale-searching, trend-spotting, franchise-hopping shopper. Spurred by Reagan's gospel of progress and prosperity, Americans happily indulged themselves. "God wants you to succeed," Reverend Robert Schuller preached from his "shopping center for God," the $19.5 million Crystal Cathedral seating three thousand.

Shopping became the great American religion, with advertising jingles uniting Americans through a common liturgy. Loudmouths in stadiums would shout "Tastes great," echoing a popular Budweiser commercial for light, spelled lite, beer. The Pavlovian crowd would respond: "Less filling!"—round after round after round. Malls sprouted like mushrooms across the landscape, creating huge, homogenized, artificial environments, killing off main streets and helping franchises gobble up individual entrepreneurs. And Americans became more obsessed than ever with having the latest, the hottest, the best—an obsession exemplified by the craze for cherubic-faced Cabbage Patch dolls, the must-get gift of Christmas 1983 that arrived with a birth certificate and hospital papers.

Reagan's rhetoric made this prosperity patriotic—and transcendent. To the millions who happily began to view the world from his perspective, Reagan's "vision thing" was more than a perception game or an exercise in image-making. A surprisingly nimble politician, Ronald Reagan understood the alchemy of leadership, especially in the modern world. More than anything else, and transcending all the president's half-steps and hypocrisies, missteps and muddles, Reagan's all-American outlook defined his times. Reaganism was liberty-laden but moralistic, consumer-oriented but idealistic, nationalist but individualistic, and consistently optimistic. Cataloguing Reagan's attributes is not enough; they must be seen in action and understood in context. Reagan's vision, this gift, demands that the two stories be told together, chronicling Ronald Reagan and America in the 1980s, the decade he dominated and helped define.

## In Search of Reagan:
## The Greatest President Since FDR?

Nearly a quarter of a century after Ronald Reagan's inauguration, Americans still have trouble discussing Reagan intelligently, objectively, reasonably. He seems easier to lionize, or demonize, than analyze. Reagan's near-canonization in June 2004 celebrated a Churchillian leader, an extraordinary character who saved America, shrinking government, restoring pride, triggering prosperity, and winning the cold war. Nevertheless, most academics and liberals charge that "Mr. Magoo," this "amiable dunce," ruined America, unleashing the evil genie of mass selfishness, while shredding the social safety nets Democratic presidents from Franklin Roosevelt through Lyndon Johnson had so carefully woven. Even as hundreds of millions worldwide heard Baroness Margaret Thatcher toast a "great president, a great American, and a great man, who, as former Canadian Prime Minister Brian Mulroney said, enters history "with certainty and panache," even while hundreds of thousands clogged the freeways of Los Angeles and the streets of Washington to salute the flag-draped coffin, others condemned Ronald Reagan's insensitivity to blacks, gays, women, and the poor. Contradicting its obituary, the *New York Times* editorial page condemned Reagan's—and his successors' "simplicity, which expresses itself in semi-detached leadership and a black-and-white view of the world."

Like him or hate him, the funeral coverage confirmed that Ronald Reagan was the greatest American president since Franklin D. Roosevelt—using the *Time* man-of-the-year standard of "the person who most affected the news and our lives, for good or for ill." Reagan's combination of visionary rigidity and tactical fluidity reinvigorated the presidency. His Hollywood-slick, small-town faith in America as a shining "city upon a hill" restored many Americans' confidence in themselves and their country. Gradually, remarkably, despite being underestimated, Reagan helped shift the terms of the debate in America. As the political scientist Aaron Wildavsky would note after Reagan's successful 1984 reelection bid against Walter Mondale: "If Mondale was so smart, and Reagan so dumb, why did the Democrats campaign on Republican issues?" Nostalgia for Reagan's courtliness and firmness elevated the fortieth president's standing in polls assessing chief executives. Even the great liberal historian Arthur Schlesinger, Jr., recently ranked Reagan with Thomas Jefferson, Andrew Jackson, and Theodore Roosevelt as "forceful and persuasive presidents" who "impose[d] their own priorities on the country," despite "the absence of first-order crisis."

Not only were Reagan's prosperity-filled, budget-busting, government-bashing, nation-building, image-making, morale-boosting, flag-waving, cold war–ending eight years defining, but Reagan and Reaganism still influence the White House, Washington, the United States, and the world. Reagan's first Democratic successor, Bill Clinton, ran for reelection in 1996 with the Reaganesque boast that "the era of big government is over," while the issue of cutting taxes was the central domestic motif for the two Bushes, who followed Reagan. Throughout the 1980s and 1990s, Americans enjoyed what we should call the Ronald Reagan–Bill Clinton presidential boom, the Paul Volcker–Alan Greenspan Federal Reserve boom, or the high tech–information age–sixties kids-reach-their-earning-potential–baby boom boom. And we are well into the second decade of Germany's peaceful reunification—part of a worldwide post-Communist democratic and capitalist revolution—

remembering that it was Reagan who challenged Gorbachev to "tear down" that wall.

All over, signs abound that, for better or worse, we live in a Reaganized America. We see it in America's emergence as the world's only superpower, and in the capitalist resurgence in the United States and abroad. We see it in how Reagan's Sun Belt conservatism continues to shine—or cast a shadow—in the courts, the Congress, and state capitals. We see it in the continuing cultural conversation about our values and souls. We see it in the blurring of popular and political culture, as prime-time television shows model themselves on White House life and create a fictional president more popular than the actual incumbent, as stars queue up for political runs to join California Governor Arnold Schwarzenegger in politics, and as presidents and their wives play the fame game like Hollywood celebrities. We see it in the polarizing effect of simple, visionary doctrines such as George W. Bush's war on terrorism, which galvanized most Americans while alienating an articulate, passionate minority. We see it in the new economy, the cutting-edge technologies, the growth in service jobs rather than manufacturing, and the debate over the gap between the richest and the poorest. We see it in the conspicuous spending that continues to consume so many of us and the unwillingness of too many of us to help the less fortunate. We see it in the continuing battles over the issues that brought Reagan to power: abortion, affirmative action, the budget, Social Security, taxes. And we see it in the sentimental patriotism that he helped revive, as evidenced by America's resolve during the Gulf War, the country's unity-in-pain after September 11, and our ever-kitschier national celebrations.

## The Reagan Treatment

Ronald Reagan was not an idiot. The need for such a declaration reflects the breadth of opinions about him—and the depths to which the debate can sink. Even his loyal wife Nancy Reagan admitted that her husband constructed a "wall" around himself. And he was remarkably, sometimes dangerously, uncurious. But that does not make Reagan "an apparent airhead," as his official biographer turned fictionalized memoirist Edmund Morris said; nor does it make him uniquely "enigmatic"—an overused term that diverts attention from Reagan's accomplishments.

Many biographers demonstrate Reagan's elusiveness by recalling the time Michael Reagan approached his father, who was officiating at the boy's graduation. Extending his hand, Governor Reagan said: "My name is Ronald Reagan, what's yours?" Michael may have felt rejected. And psychobiographers can revel in such stunning indifference to one's child. But there is a more benign explanation. The progressive journalist William Allen White noted that after years in politics, William McKinley "became galvanized with a certain coating of publicity. He lost his private life and his private view. . . . He walked among men a bronze statue, for thirty years determinedly looking for his pedestal." Decades as a Hollywood star and a politician conditioned Reagan to retreat into a shell while in public, to play his part without being engaged. The Michael Reagan incident may indicate the coping mechanisms of a celebrity imprisoned within his own "galvanized . . . coating" rather than revealing a uniquely "enigmatic" man.

In fact, Ronald Reagan's political career relied on his first-class temperament. His light touch, his affable manner, the sparkle in his eyes telegraphed a warmth that belied claims he was a right-wing bogeyman. Without his conservative grounding, Reagan would have floated away; without the image-making, he would have sunk under the weight of his rhetoric. Reagan's optimism was heartfelt and legendary, springing from his faith in America, the resilient, innocent era that nurtured him, and his storybook rise from the shame of having a drunken, ineffectual father and a religiously iconoclastic mother in small-town USA to Hollywood fame and presidential immortality. Reagan was a great deflector, ready to blame the media, the Russians, or individuals, but rarely taking failures upon himself. When his first wife left him, he said "I *was* divorced," dodging responsibility; when the Iran-Contra scandal exploded, he bemoaned the journalistic "lynch mob" that "prevented the remaining hostages from being released."

Even opponents often succumbed to the Reagan charm. If Lyndon Johnson's infamous "treatment" entailed hovering, dominating, invading his victim's space, with an implicit threat reinforcing the physical intrusion, the Reagan treatment was more subtle, minimalist, Mc-Luhanesque. This president lured, appeased, and distracted, inviting his victim into his charmed circle, his can-do worldview, all reinforced with a well-aimed anecdote or witticism. Reagan believed in getting people to "love you, not just believe you," in public and in private. "I think I gained that knowledge in show business," he said, "and out on the road I do my very best to establish a personal relationship—even with a crowd. It's easy for me, too, because the truth of the matter is I do like people."

## Ronald Reagan's Bully Pulpit

Reagan was a great teacher, an extraordinary preacher, a master of parables, conveying complex ideas in short, friendly soundbites that stirred the American soul. Reagan worked his magic as America's favorite storyteller, improvising a narrative about the present and the future rooted in Americans' mythic past. Although his policies sometimes proved divisive, he is best appreciated as a harmonizer, a fabulist who reconciled apparent contradictions, a sentimentalist surprisingly adept at forging unlikely coalitions. And for all the talk about the Reagan "Revolution," the president often played the pragmatist, not the ideologue; the politician, not the idealist.

Reagan delighted in Theodore Roosevelt's "bully pulpit." Inspiring the masses while infuriating his critics, he spoke impressionistically, telegraphically, and sometimes inaccurately. Reagan and his aides tended to value salesmanship over statesmanship, trusting "the Talent's" ability to woo the public. Criticized by women, attacked by blacks, Reagan's aides worked harder to "communicate our present attitudes"—without reconsidering policies.

Reagan's impressionism worked because he sounded so sincere. *Newsweek*'s Meg Greenfield marveled at Reagan's "gift" of "saying the most incredible things" credibly. In 1982 Reagan told Chicago school kids that the British used to hang criminals for possessing guns. Reporters jeered. Echoing his boss's approach, Deputy Press Secretary Larry Speakes replied: "Well, it's a good story, though. It made the point, didn't it?"

Reagan defended himself from accusations of inaccuracy with his characteristic mix of populism, self-assurance, and good humor. "I have never claimed to be a whiz kid, a robot, a bionic adding machine, or a walking encyclopedia," he said, using quaint language in the computer age to identify with the masses and mock the elites. With the self-assurance of old age, Reagan impressed other world leaders by shrugging off criticism. He was who he was, Canada's Brian Mulroney later recalled. Unlike many younger, thin-skinned leaders, Reagan was not a work in progress. The smooth, affable showman enjoyed laughing at himself. When opponents attacked the air force's costly B-1 bomber, he quipped: "How did I know it was an airplane? I thought it was vitamins for the troops."

Rather than rethinking liberal fundamentals, Democrats preferred to caricature Reagan as a lucky boob whose public relations elixir bewitched Americans. The result was a series of Reagan "upsets," from his election in November 1980, through his string of congressional successes in 1981, through his reelection in 1984, and including his managing of Mikhail Gorbachev and the twilight of Communism. Reagan made a career of being underestimated—thanks to the arrogance of Democrats and reporters.

In fact, Reagan had more depth. Thousands of documents housed in the Ronald Reagan Presidential Library prove that Ronald Reagan was a thinker, a writer, an engaged politician. For decades he drafted his own speeches—and he remained his own best speechwriter. Even as crushing presidential workloads reduced him to editing his ghostwriters' drafts, Reagan often substituted vivid prose for policy jargon, powerful yarns for broad principles, inclusive "we" language rather than distancing abstractions. Similarly, the White House lobbying records reveal the relish with which Reagan did his "homework," calling up members of Congress, arm-twisting gently, and diligently recording the results.

Reagan's White House was uniquely positioned to exploit some profound cultural changes. Theodore Roosevelt's turn-of-the-century bully pulpit had become the late twentieth century's most formidable sound stage. Democrats such as Franklin D. Roosevelt and John F. Kennedy, Republicans such as Dwight Eisenhower and Richard Nixon, had expanded, invigorated, and wired the presidency. Dominating the federal government and the media, the president became the focal point of the country, not just its politics. The White House offered one of America's most effective backdrops; for one who could appreciate its potential, being president was the greatest public role. Reagan brought to this souped-up soapbox an ease with the cameras, a fluidity of formal speech, an ear for popular concerns, an instinct for mass leadership, and an appreciation for the presidency's public relations power. The 1980s would be Reagan's decade because Reagan skillfully rode and often took credit for one independently generated cultural wave after another, ranging from the founding of CNN, MTV, and *USA Today*, to the reign of *Dallas* and *Dynasty* on television, and the transition from Walter Cronkite to Dan Rather at CBS News—all of which occurred at the start of Reagan's administration.

Conservatives bristle at characterizations of their hero's accomplishments as largely symbolic, especially because it feeds the liberal caricature of Reagan as a snake-oil salesman. But, particularly in the modern American polity, symbolic leadership is significant. Tone counts. The "Rhetorical Presidency" lives and thrives. When many historians talk about the idealism John F. Kennedy inspired in the 1960s, they wax lyrical. Yet when many talk about the song Reagan sang, they turn cynical. Obviously, differences in content remain relevant. But neither liberals nor conservatives should underestimate the modern president's power to shape the nation's self-perception and worldview, or the centrality of that mission in molding an administration's legacy.

## Reagan's Poetic Politics:
## Merging Politics *and* Culture

From the perspective of the early twenty-first century, the 1980s loom large. During that decade the information age began, spawning a new economy, a new politics, a new culture, a new look, and a new flight from communal concerns to individual lifestyle obsessions. Examining the 1980s illuminates how our contemporary world was shaped—and distorted.

Presidential historians have underestimated the cultural impact presidents have, especially in the modern age. This book builds on this assumption, that to understand Ronald Reagan—and the era he dominated—we need to recognize Reagan's presidency as a cultural and political phenomenon. More so than his predecessors, and building on the examples of Franklin D. Roosevelt and John F. Kennedy, Reagan's brand of leadership partially transcended day-to-day politics and helped shape American culture. Presidents continue to captivate America's collective psyche, and a president like Reagan, who set out to resurrect the grandeur of his nation and his office, remains especially intriguing.

Armed with his easy grin, his sunny disposition, and an array of anecdotes trumpeting traditional American values, Reagan repeatedly merged culture and politics. Reagan's boundary jumping entailed more than the occasional Clint Eastwood or Rambo reference that came so easily to the former Hollywood star. In his preference for storytelling over policy-making, in his tendency to paper over divisive issues with unifying themes, in his poetic politics of symbols and images trumping the Jimmy Carter–Tip O'Neill prosaic politics of logrolling and coalition building, Ronald Reagan brought to life the academic notion of "political culture." Reagan "was a performer in an era when we were only beginning to realize that performing was one of the most important things a presidential candidate could do," notes Roger Simon of *U.S. News & World Report*. Reagan demonstrated that politics was more than a power game and a question of resource allocation, it often involved a clash of symbols and a collective search for meaning.

Reagan's gruff political consultant Ed Rollins called his boss "the last American hero." This label captured the president's outsized status in many American eyes as well as the nostalgia-laden fear of the complicated present that Reagan tapped into so effectively. Reagan became a hero by helping to restore America's confidence, which then helped insulate him from some of the vicissitudes that weakened his predecessors—and helped distract Americans from some of his greatest fiascos, including the Iran-Contra scandal. This model of cultural leadership, with the larger Reagan storyline eclipsing the prosaic and sometimes tawdry details of the Reagan presidency, accounted for Reagan's "teflon" that so mystified and frustrated his critics.

## The Reagan Storyline

Assessing the politics and the culture of the times uncovers a Reagan storyline. It is a simple story, told repeatedly, divided into three parts. The first part tells the sad tale of America in the 1960s and 1970s, a country demoralized, wracked by inflation, strangled by big government, humiliated by Iranian fundamentalists, outmaneuvered by Soviet communists, betrayed by its best educated and most affluent youth. The result was four failed presidents: Lyndon Johnson, Richard Nixon, Gerald Ford, and Jimmy Carter. Part two has Ronald Reagan riding in to save the day, with a mandate for change. Reagan's relentless, eloquent, often soaring rhetoric reshaped American horizons, building on century-old ideals, responding to decades-old frustrations, utilizing the challenges of the moment. His revolution, in his telling, lightened the tax burden crushing Americans, cut many regulatory shackles handcuffing American business, and revived America's military. Just as Franklin D. Roosevelt's National Recovery Administration played to the consumer, the businessman, and the worker, Ronald Reagan's America in recovery played to the citizen, the businessman, and the soldier. The result, part three, was Morning in America—the great party known as the 1980s, when the stock market soared, patriotism surged, the Soviet Union crumbled, and America thrived.

Reagan and his minions delighted in this tale. They told it so frequently, and so brazenly, that they alienated some fellow Republicans, who occupied the White House from 1969 to 1977. Nixon and Ford administration veterans bristled when President Reagan called the 1970s a "decade of neglect," a time when "those in charge seemed to be operating under the notion that a weaker America is a more secure America." "I resent being lumped in with Carter and the Democratic Congresses on this vital issue," Gerald Ford scolded two former subordinates now working for Reagan in 1984—Vice President George Bush and Chief of Staff James Baker.

This Reagan storyline of decay and renaissance was all the more remarkable given its tenuous relationship to the truth. Ronald Reagan's two terms were not the eight-year idyll many now recall. Reagan's revolution was not as dramatic as many now claim, and the morning in America was not as cloud free. Even Reagan's poll ratings were not that consistently high. In particular, the Reagan recession of 1981 to 1982 generated the most unemployment since the Great Depression; midway through Reagan's first term, pundits were eulogizing yet another failed administration. Even at the height of the Reagan boom, serious questions lingered about the mounting debt, about the growing gap between rich and poor, about the fraying of Reagan's vaunted "safety net," about the threat of Japanese and German economic dominance. And even once Reagan's poll ratings recovered, pollsters consistently discovered far more affection for the man than support for his policies.

## The 1980s: A Meeting of the Man and the Moment

Historians have long pondered the dynamics between historical actors and forces, between, as they used to say, the man and the moment. Arthur M. Schlesinger, Jr., wonders what would have happened had the assassin who killed Chicago's Mayor Anton Cermak in February 1933 hit his target, President-elect Roosevelt, and had the automobile that merely bruised England's future prime minister crossing Fifth Avenue fourteen months earlier crushed Winston Churchill. Historians are not supposed to play counterfactual games, but one leap prompts another. Suppose Ronald Reagan had wrested the Republican nomination from President Gerald Ford in 1976, and then defeated Jimmy Carter. Would a Reagan presidency beginning in 1977 have been as effective? Reagan would have imposed the same ideas, habits, and personality on a country that was less confident economically, strategically, culturally, ideologically. To the extent that Reagan benefited by playing off Carter, the malaise talk, the Iranian hostage debacle, and the general frustration pent up during the Ford-Carter years; to the extent that a show like *Dynasty* went into production in 1979 and not in 1975; to the extent that the "USA USA" cheering after the plucky

American team's surprising Olympic hockey victory occurred in 1980, Reagan may have been lucky to lose in 1976.

Reagan was not the first president to be funny, eloquent, patriotic, or even optimistic. His supposedly malaise-ridden predecessor, Jimmy Carter, sported a million-watt smile and the confidence-inducing slogan, "Why Not the Best?" During the 1977 inauguration, Carter called for "a new beginning, a new dedication without our Government, and a new spirit among us all." Yet Carter warned, prophetically: "A President may sense and proclaim that new spirit, but only a people can provide it." Ronald Reagan was not simply lucky in getting the American people to "provide" that new spirit in the 1980s, he was sufficiently savvy to turn whatever coincidences came along the way into his—and America's—good fortune.

Reagan's extraordinary skills found fertile soil and the right political climate, at the right time. The economy improved. Deregulation intensified. The baby boomers matured. Corporations became more popular. Soviet Communism imploded. Meanwhile, media attention shifted from liberal suburbanites' rebellion against the authoritarian establishment and stultifying conformity to conservative suburbanites' rebellion against big government and high taxes. Ronald Reagan's message resonated more effectively. His ability to hijack historical forces, and define them, improved.

Reagan's governing style suited this new society and political culture obsessed with the pursuit of happiness. It was low-impact governing, minimizing demands and mass-producing happy endings. Reagan served out dollops of traditional American fare promising limited government and maximal salvation in modern, media-friendly packages. A politics of postures and images, alternating with a focus on a few discrete issues that engaged him fully, stirred an audience exhausted by the grandiose promises of yesteryear and distracted by *Entertainment Tonight*. Ronald Reagan was remarkably chipper, even-keeled, friendly, happy to trade jokes and quips. Biographers can deem this persona enigmatic and problematic; most Americans found it alluring and reassuring. Reagan's compulsive affability fed an optimism that also resonated with Americans, who were desperate for can-do, upbeat leadership after the traumas of the 1960s and the anxieties of the 1970s. And along with this affability and optimism came a great faith in the American experiment. Ronald Reagan's old-fashioned patriotism shaped both his anti-Communism and his broad, inclusive, seductive vision that in 1984 would be summarized in the campaign ad celebrating "Morning again in America."

This optimism and pro-Americanism forged a governing template useful to future presidents from both sides of the aisle. Ronald Reagan taught Bill Clinton and George W. Bush the importance of big-picture governing, of integrating cultural and political leadership, of shaping a transcendent narrative that could insulate the president from the inevitable missteps and even larger scandals and errors. One cannot understand how Bill Clinton survived the Monica Lewinsky scandal, how George W. Bush thrived after September 11, without first understanding Ronald Reagan's model of presidential leadership.

Unfortunately, the results of this alchemy with the American people were often mixed. There was a sense in the 1980s of "Morning in America," as the economy soared, the Soviet Union faltered, and American patriotism surged. But there was mourning in America, too, as the social pathologies of crime, drugs, ghettoization, failing schools, family breakdown, and ineffectual immigration policies persisted along with a growing superficiality and selfishness, even hard-heartedness, as the wealthy seemed to reap Reagan's bounty disproportionately.

Ronald Reagan's 1980s was the decade of supply-side economics, the Laffer curve, and budget-slashing politics, of tax cuts, regulatory freezes, the Evil Empire, and defense hikes, when arcane talk about balancing the budget and the reconciliation process became regular dinner table fare. "Big government" was the problem, not the solution; it was something to "get off our backs" rather than to protect us or bring into our lives. Liberals, bureaucrats, and special interests were bad; a safety net and entitlements for the "truly needy" were acceptable; businessmen, budget-cutters, and the Moral Majority were good. Thanks to Reagan, and the first Republican Senate since 1954, in fact the first Republican House of Congress in almost thirty years, the Republicans defined much of the political agenda for the coming two decades.

## The 1980s: Gilded and Guilty or
## Renewed and Reaganite?

The Reagan mourning rites revealed that two competing stereotypes shape public discussion of the 1980s. When politicians and pop culture impresarios refer to "the eighties," they usually mean the vapid, hedonistic, amoral years of America's new gilded age, when yuppies reigned and greed was good. Perpetuated today in eighties' parties and in movies such as Adam Sandler's *The Wedding Singer,* the eighties' stereotype recalls Wall Street excess and political selfishness; an era when junk bonds and trashy values created deficits "as far as the eye could see" and triggered the multibillion-dollar Savings and Loan crisis. Rogues who defined the times include jailed moguls such as Ivan Boesky and Leona Helmsley; disgraced ministers such as Jim Bakker and Jimmy Swaggart. In 1992 Bill Clinton ran for president against this version of the 1980s. "The Reagan-Bush years have exalted private gain over public obligations, special interests over common good, wealth and fame over work and family," Clinton charged when launching his campaign. "The 1980s ushered in a gilded age of greed, selfishness, irresponsibility, excess, and neglect."

Yet when Ronald Reagan died, most of the press and public defined the same era as one of renewal and idealism, of national unity and glory. A collective act of national amnesia ignored how reporters mocked Reagan, how Democrats like Senator Edward Kennedy blasted his "unilateral," militaristic, reckless, and divisive foreign policy, how hundreds of thousands of Europeans protested against the president repeatedly. Most Europeans deemed him, Professor Michael Mandelbaum reported in 1985, "ill equipped for the responsibility that he bears, a kind of cowboy figure, bellicose, ignorant, with a simplistic view of the world pieced together from the journals of right-wing opinion and old Hollywood movies." Instead, two decades later, one letter the *New York Times* printed recalled "a simpler time . . . when all things seemed possible and Americans felt good about their country." In eulogizing Reagan, President George W. Bush endorsed the "great man" theory of history, calling the Reaganized eighties "one of the decisive decades of the century as the convictions that shaped the president began to shape the times." *Time*'s commemorative issue claimed the Reagan era created "an America that is stronger militarily, more dedicated to free enterprise, more mindful of the virtues of self-reliance and more confident in its own powers." Even Bill Clinton, now an ex-president, said Reagan "personified the indomitable optimism of the American people" and kept "America at the forefront of the fight for freedom for people everywhere."

Clearly, the political fights of the 1980s persisted into the twenty-first century. "To conservatives, 1980 is the year one," CNN's Bill Schneider explained. But Ronald Reagan's conservative utopia for some created a liberal dystopia for others. "I think the world would have been better off if he had not been President," the AIDS activist and playwright Larry Kramer told *People*.

This book tries to go beyond the clashing oversimplifications of both the "eighties' decadence" and "Reagan renewal" stereotypes. In fact, America would have to wait a decade—and silence the Democratic opposition by electing a Democratic president—for this "eighties"-style cultural revolution to proceed unchecked. In many ways, Bill Clinton's rollicking, hedonistic 1990s became what many social critics feared Ronald Reagan's 1980s would be.

To the extent that Reaganism helped paved the way for Clintonism, Reagan succeeded by being trendy rather than countercultural. Despite Reagan's traditionalism, his faith in individualism and his passive nature mostly furthered the various social and cultural revolutions he disliked. Even while believing they were choosing the old-fashioned way, Americans ratified many social changes by incorporating them into their lives. It was often an unhappy fit, sending indices of social pathology and individual misery soaring, yet Americans were acclimating to many of these problems. Increasingly "the underclass," the "teen-suicide epidemic," and "family breakdown" were becoming familiar, static phenomena rather than crises to be solved.

Overall, Reagan's 1980s accelerated the social solvents he blamed on the 1960s and 1970s. Going from the "Me Decade" to the "Mine All Mine Decade," citizens in Reagan's America felt less engaged, less constrained, less interdependent than ever. In the individualism he worshiped, the hypocrisy he embodied, and the politicization of moral discourse he facilitated, Reagan further undermined the traditional collective mores he so proudly hailed. And as more of a compromiser than a revolutionary on social issues, he continued to institutionalize some of the changes. Most liberals were too busy demonizing Reaganite "greed" and blindly defending the 1960s, big government, and anything Reagan opposed to notice, while most conservatives were simply too busy defending their hero just as blindly.

Nevertheless, throughout the 1980s, and subsequently, critics from the Left and the Right mourned America's growing "decadence," and some recognized that Reagan helped leach America's "social capital," pollute America's "social ecology," and diminish Americans' sense of citizenship and community. This process of communal fragmentation had been developing throughout the twentieth century, from the hedonism of the 1920s' flappers to the atomism of the 1950s' corporate drone. Yet in the 1980s it seemed to have reached the tipping point. After the social revolutions of the 1960s and 1970s, the process of decitizenization, if you will, seemed more ubiquitous, more blatant, less reversible. That this untrammelled individualism and resulting anomie came wrapped in a red-white-and-blue package, delivered by an old-fashioned gentleman distinguished by his midwestern courtliness and all-American idealism, accompanied by America's great cold war victory and the world's turn from flirting with socialism to appreciating capitalism, fed the clashing stereotypes and interpretive confusion.

## A Watershed Decade: Where the 1960s and the 1980s Meet

Looking back, then, the 1980s emerge as a watershed decade, a time when the Great Reconciliation between Reaganite conservatism and 1960s' liberalism occurred. For all the talk about repudiating the New Deal, dismantling the Great Society, and undoing the 1960s' social and cultural revolutions, many innovations became routinized and institutionalized. The tone changed, Americans overall felt less mopey and less gloomy, less idealistic and more materialistic, but the melodies lingered on, from environmentalism to feminism, from the rights revolution to the continuing revolt against authority. Reagan, at heart, was not a revolutionary. He was more a conciliator than a reformer, to the frustration of ideologues like David Stockman and to the great relief of many others.

Surprisingly, Reagan's moderate traditionalism provided cover both for the decadence of the age and for the vitality of many 1960s-style revolutions. Progressives mourned the death of the sixties even as the 1980s consolidated many of the most dramatic lifestyle transformations. Yes, the civil rights movement seemed to falter, but Jesse Jackson ran for president, Michael Jackson dominated the music world, Bill Cosby revived the TV sitcom, Oprah Winfrey became an American icon, and, most important, millions of blacks entered the professions, moved into good neighborhoods, received better educations, and progressed. Even AIDS, the deadly scourge neglected for too long by President Reagan and too many gay leaders, ultimately helped mainstream gay life and highlight America's scientific wizardry.

The 1960s continues to define the baby boom generation just as the Depression and World War II defined the boomers' parents. Reagan wanted to confront the legacy of the 1960s. Reagan himself did not realize—and would never acknowledge—just how many aspects of the 1960s he and his comrades either aped or incorporated. From the way the conservative movement mimicked some of the 1960s' "movement culture," to the mainstreaming of granola and blue jeans, of Naderism and environmentalism, the 1980s did more to advance the sixties agenda, such as it was, than to dismantle it, especially culturally.

Some of the intensity of the sixties' movement, combined with the ferocity of the anti-Reaganite opposition, morphed into the 1980s' identity politics and political correctness. Here, too, a great mystery persists. Even critics usually acknowledge Reagan's role in resurrecting American patriotism and restoring some American consensus. And yet the 1980s also spawned movements rejecting the fundamentals of American identity, as European postmodernist ideas overran the universities and insinuated themselves into the media, Hollywood, and much of the Northeastern and Californian elite.

At the same time, in the 1980s American capitalism and entrepreneurship rallied. The 1970s' economic failures—notably in the automobile industry—were repaired in the 1980s. And the technological innovations that would shape the 1990s' boom developed in the 1980s. Microwave ovens, videocassette recorders, facsimile machines, and personal computers were beginning to revolutionize the American economy and the American home. The titans of "the new economy," the Microsofts, MCIs, Sprints, Intels, and Time-Warners, were forming, merging, consolidating, growing.

Reagan's renewal, such as it was, was not simply economic or political. It was ideological, cultural, and philosophical, too. Reagan's bedrock faith not just in America, but in God and in a higher purpose to life, recalled the Founding Fathers' simple, not very ritualistic, deism. While Reagan did not attend church regularly, he said he prayed frequently—and believed deeply. Similarly, Reagan's anti-Communism was more than reactionary. His embrace of capitalism, democracy, and freedom itself stemmed from a broader philosophy of history. As President George W. Bush recognized in eulogizing Reagan, "The ideology he opposed throughout his political life insisted that history was moved by impersonal tides and unalterable fates. Ronald Reagan believed instead in the courage and triumph of free men, and we believe it all the more because we saw that courage in him."

Before the eighties' stereotype petrifies, historians sensitive to the complexities must reevaluate that decade. Rather than condemning the eighties as a new Gilded Age when the wealthy partied and the poor languished, rather than worshiping the era as a conservative Golden Age when America united and good triumphed, it is more illuminating to speak of an Era of Good Feelings, when most Americans felt better about themselves and their country, thanks partially to Ronald Reagan. Feelings are ephemeral and idiosyncratic. And the happy mood did not always comport with reality—or prove enduring. Nevertheless, that optimism, trusting that America was following the right track and fulfilling the right ideals, set the cultural tone.

## Defining a Decade of Ordinary Life:
## Only Yesterday, and Today

Although all historical writing has been described as trying to nail Jello to a wall, writing a book like this is particularly daunting. How can one dare define a decade, a year, a moment in the life of this raucous and wonderful collection of a quarter-billion souls? Reviewing the previous decade from his vantage point in 1931 in *Only Yesterday,* the journalist Frederick Lewis Allen described the "ordinary" day a "typical" middle-class American family, the Smiths, experienced in May 1919. Using the same technique to look at January 20, 1981, Ronald Reagan's inaugural, also proves illuminating. This Mr. and Mrs. Smith would follow a fashion timetable similar to their grandparents'. Mr. Smith's standard business suit would not change much over the decade, although in 1981 he would never consider wearing a shirt with a different-colored collar. Mrs. Smith would experience more dramatic fashion upheavals. At work, she wore Halston suits to command respect; at home, she might slip into her Calvin Klein jeans, amused by those who objected to fifteen-year-old Brooke Shields cooing in a commercial: "You know what comes between me and my Calvins? Nothing." CBS had banned the ad.

Mr. and Mrs. Smith would drive to work in Japanese cars, having soured on American gas-guzzlers. In the office, both Mr. and Mrs. Smith would monitor the continuing effects of stagflation, the one-two punch of unemployment and inflation, with soaring interest rates.

The Smiths would struggle home through rush hour traffic, despite leaving considerably after five, and pick up some ethnic variety of take-out food on the way home. Their door would have a double lock—added after a recent rash of break-ins. They would each have a beer—increasingly an imported or domestic specialty brand—or share a bottle of California wine, their pot-smoking days over, although some friends occasionally snorted cocaine at weekend parties. After watching CBS News with Walter Cronkite, they would settle down for an evening of prime-time TV—mostly viewing shows on the three dominant networks, CBS, NBC, and ABC. Lacking a remote-control TV, they would drift off to sleep with the television droning, with the channel set to their local NBC affiliate, for Johnny Carson's melange of one-liners, zany antics, and celebrity guests, punctuated by Ed McMahon's sycophantic guffaws. Hipper and more insomniac couples would have to wait until 1982 before *Late Night with David Letterman* premiered, in the slot an hour later.

Unlike their grandparents, Mr. and Mrs. Smith used birth control to postpone the start of their family, so both could solidify their careers and save for their starter house in the suburbs. Thanks to the great inflation, DINKS like them, double incomes, no kids, were buying simple four-bedroom houses from blue-collar retirees with stay-at-home wives. "The older generation had it easy," the Smiths often thought, sobered by the $300,000 cost of a house their parents could have purchased decades ago for one-tenth that amount.

About half their friends were married—one couple having recently separated just as the husband finished his medical training. Mrs. Smith worried about her single female friends who despaired about their long-term prospects. Mr. Smith's bachelor buddies seemed carefree.

If the Smiths voted in the 1980 election, and barely half of their fellow Americans did, they probably voted for Ronald Reagan. However, they were more disappointed by Jimmy Carter than wowed by Reagan, and they briefly considered voting for the independent John Anderson. Mr. Smith wondered if an actor had the gravitas to govern, and Mrs. Smith feared Reagan might be too bellicose with the Soviets and too harsh on the poor. Both voted for their incumbent Democratic congressman to temper Reagan's Revolution. By January, perceptions of the incoming president shifted, with less talk about his Hollywood background or doctrinaire anti-Communism, and more celebrations of his confidence and patriotism, which seemed contagious. Even if neither would ever fully embrace his program, the Smiths were warming up to this fatherly figure, and happily bid farewell to Carter.

In 1981 these people would still think of Apple as a fruit, not a computer; of "power ties" as electric lines, not fashion statements; of Madonna as a theological figure, not a celebrity; of Sonny Bono as a rock star, not a politician; of *The Big Chill* as blowing in from Canada, not Hollywood; of "greenmail" as a colorful letter, not a predatory financial tactic; of a secretary, not a fancy tape recorder, as an answering machine. AIDS would sound like helpers, not a scourge; Iran-Contra would sound like a folk dance with a Mideastern twist, not a scandal; a salad bar would sound like a contradiction in terms; and Boy George would evoke thoughts of the first U.S. president when he was young and menacing cherry trees.

*Miami Vice* would not sound suitable for polite company. CNN, MTV, ESPN, and VCR would mean nothing, with PC meaning neither a personal computer nor politically correct. Rapping meant communicating intensely or tapping lightly, not chanting rhythmically; a mouse squeaked but did not click; windows broke but did not crash; people wore boots but could not reboot. California Adonises surfed, television couch potatoes didn't. Trump referred to bridge, not buildings. The Berlin Wall was up, the stock market down. The Supreme Court was all male. And America's most famous Turners were Ike and Tina, not Ted.

This book examines some of these phenomena that defined millions of American lives, analyzing what stayed constant and what changed—and why. Each chapter will focus on a particular year from 1980 to 1990, emphasizing themes that defined that year. Most chapters begin in a particular location, illustrating the theme while testifying to the nation's diversity. The resulting portrait shows how Ronald Reagan dominated the 1980s, while also showing that this decade, like so many others in our history, was a time of high drama, great progress, and intense frustration—a time when more people than ever before fulfilled the American dream, but many of us, in true American fashion, from the Left and the Right, realized it was not yet enough—and justifiably demanded liberty and justice and equality and prosperity and meaning and morality and community for all.

# 1980

## Cleveland

### "There You Go Again!"
### Defeating Defeatism—and Jimmy Carter

---

> I would like to be president, because I would like to see this
> country become once again a country where a little six-year-old
> girl can grow up knowing the same freedom that I knew
> when I was six years old, growing up in America.
>
> RONALD REAGAN, CAMPAIGN SPEECH, 1976

Even though he was president of the United States, the most powerful man on earth, Jimmy Carter was nervous. True, he dismissed his opponent, Ronald Reagan, as a lightweight. But three weeks before the November 1980 presidential election, the numbers were looking soft.

It had not been an easy twelve months, with the crown prince of Camelot, Senator Edward Kennedy, challenging Carter for the Democratic Party nomination, the Iranians kidnapping American diplomats, the Russians invading Afghanistan, the military failing to free the hostages, and special prosecutors investigating brother Billy's lobbying for Libya. Besides, American morale was down, and the economy was plummeting. Inflation and interest rates were soaring—both were in the double digits.

The presidential debate was taking place in Cleveland, Ohio, a symbol of America's ills. Once Cleveland was one of the Northeast's many jewels, a glittering gem on that prosperous, productive I-90 necklace circling the Great Lakes along with Syracuse, Rochester, Buffalo, Toledo, and Chicago. Now "the mistake by the lake," like its sister cities, was a sad punchline, another disaster area. "What is the difference between Cleveland and the Titanic?" wags asked. "Cleveland has a better orchestra." Cleveland suffered all the urban Rust Belt diseases—crime, racial conflict, decaying infrastructure, "deindustrialization," pollution. In 1969 the Cuyahoga River, brimming with chemical gunk, burst into flame, epitomizing the Northeast's decline.

The presidency had aged Jimmy Carter. Still healthy at fifty-three, over a decade younger than his Republican rival, Carter jogged, played tennis, swam, hunted, fished—when he had time. But his face, newly creased, wore the burdens of office. His brown hair had grayed considerably.

Carter looked like a pinched parson in his severe Sunday suit during his ninety-minute debate with Ronald Reagan. He occasionally bared his teeth, but the grimace was nothing like the full-toothed million-watt smile that defined his Cinderella-like rise to power in 1976. During the debate, straining to appear folksy, he invoked his daughter Amy when advocating nuclear arms limitations. But Americans were not ready to consult a thirteen-year-old girl regarding global strategy. The perfectionist, usually unflappable president ended his flaccid performance by thanking "the people of Cleveland and Ohio for being such hospitable hosts during these last few hours *in* my life"—his syntax suggesting he was facing the executioner, not the electorate.

By contrast, Ronald Reagan triumphed that October night. After stumbling early on in Iowa, Reagan had run a smooth primary effort. The general campaign began with some gaffes, as the candidate seemed to endorse creationism, praised Vietnam as a "noble cause"— which would sound less controversial a decade later—and suggested that trees generate more air pollution than cars. Despite the occasional protest sign picturing a tree saying "Stop me before I kill again," Reagan had shrugged off the errors and plunged ahead.

Reagan was an accomplished showman, a veteran actor who could not understand how anyone could master modern politics without a show business background. Reagan's ease set a winning contrast to the president's stiffness. When Carter attacked, Reagan shook his head, kindly, condescendingly, more sad than angry, and dispatched the incumbent president by laughing off the criticism, saying, "There you go again."

Even though many liberals grumbled that Jimmy Carter governed from the right, even though many conservatives grumbled that Ronald Reagan moderated his views to win, this election offered Americans a dramatic choice. It was not just a contrast between Reagan's affability and Carter's intensity, between the actor and the engineer. Rather, the two candidates had contradictory diagnoses of America's problems—and clashing cures. Jimmy Carter was steeped in 1970s' pessimism—or realism—deeming America's problems complex, and its resources limited. Still, he trusted government to help Americans overcome. Ronald Reagan was the candidate of 1950s' optimism, confident that the people who framed the Constitution, settled the West, freed the slaves, industrialized the continent, and crushed the Nazis could solve any problem. But Reagan believed that government was part of the problem, not the solution.

"I've learned that only the most complex and difficult tasks come before me in the Oval Office. No easy answers are found there—because no easy questions come there," Carter said in his acceptance speech in New York City, itself a symbol of America's age of complexity. To Reagan, such thinking was defeatist and un-American. Reagan "utterly reject[ed]" the view "that the future will be one of sacrifice and few opportunities." Speaking a month before Carter in Chicago, rooting himself in America's heartland, and his own all-American, small-town Illinois hometown a short drive away, Reagan proclaimed: "The American people, the most generous on earth, who created the highest standard of living, are not going to accept the notion that we can only make a better world for others by moving backwards ourselves. Those who believe we *can* have no business leading this nation."

Both candidates pitched the campaign as a referendum on the 1970s, and a referendum on the new conservative ideology evolving from the older, prickly, less user-friendly 1960s' Barry Goldwater take-it-or-leave-it, we-need-extremism-in-defense-of-liberty variety. The winner of such a clash of opposites would naturally proclaim a broad mandate. And it was not easy to push Ohio and New York, Massachusetts and Minnesota into the Republican column as part of Reagan's forty-four-state sweep. Yet in 1980 the electoral verdict was less clear. Even as Ronald Reagan campaigned on the contrasts, even as he promised to return Cleveland and other American communities in crisis to a golden age, even as he forged a potentially revolutionary coalition, this shrewd politician and his aides banked on riding an anti-Carter wave into the White House.

## The 1970s: America Unmoored—and Unhappy

It made sense to build a strategy around rejecting Carter, for Americans were grouchy in 1980. Too many Americans saw too many Cleveland-like pathologies too close to their own homes. Potential voters seemed unhappy with Carter, Reagan, and the independent maverick, Illinois Congressman John Anderson. It had been a rough decade. It was not just the litany of traumas Carter mentioned in his acceptance: "the civil rights revolution, the bitterness of Vietnam, the shame of Watergate, the twilight peace of nuclear terror." The 1970s was a time of political drift, international weakness, moral upheaval, and economic disaster. Carter's "misery index" from 1976, combining inflation and unemployment, nearly doubled in four years from 12.5 to over 20. When the campaign began in September, the annual inflation rate was 22.3 percent, the prime rate at 11.25 percent. As the inflation rate, the unemployment rate, and the divorce rate all soared, American confidence plummeted.

The 1970s should have been a great time for Americans, a time when the promise of the 1960s was fulfilled and a "time to heal," in President Gerald R. Ford's words, from the previous decade. The civil disorder of the students' revolt had ended. America of the 1970s had many new programs, policies, philosophies, and practices to improve life. The civil rights movement had triumphed. Grassroots action, Supreme Court decisions, and political leadership had dismantled the ugly Jim Crow structure oppressing blacks and trapping southerners in a vicious, defensive politics of yesteryear. The Great Society was a fact of life, fighting poverty, advancing education, building housing, welcoming immigrants, protecting the environment. Détente had begun.

The United States was negotiating with its formerly unapproachable Communist adversaries, the Soviet Union and China. Moreover, women were empowered, gays galvanized, youth energized. Americans were freer than ever to express themselves, to follow their destinies, to explore their inner selves, to indulge sensual whims. Clothing was looser and more informal, sex more casual and more available, leisure more ubiquitous and more stimulating. Life itself was easier, blessed by a host of technological and pharmaceutical facilitators, from the pill to the calculator, from the digital clock to the microwave oven.

Instead, a great pall, a spectre of failure, a fear of disaster haunted American society. Civil rights had degenerated from seemingly clear black and white issues to a morass of competing choices over busing, housing, jobs, and college admissions. The Great Society was bogged down in bureaucracy, generating taxes and regulations rather than guaranteeing social justice. Détente had dissolved into an alphabet soup of acronyms, with SALT treaties to manage MIRVs and ICBMs, even as the Soviet Union appeared more aggressive than before. And amid all the leisure, all the liberation, all the toys, all the questing, and all the ESTing, many individuals were worrying, families were imploding, communities were exploding, and the nation seemed adrift.

Individual anxiety mirrored and intensified the sense of communal failure. It was not just the once almighty dollar's eroding purchasing power. It was not just the declining sense of political power. Rather, the great liberation movements of the 1960s had left many Americans feeling unmoored. The process of redefining the roles of husbands and wives, parents and children was wrenching. The sexual revolution, and its noxious partner, the divorce revolution, disrupted countless lives. In the 1970s the number of men living alone doubled, as millions of husbands responded to *Time* covers trumpeting divorce and no-fault divorce laws by breaking up families. "One million American children lost their families to divorce in each year of the 1970s," the journalist David Frum notes, "but the experts counseled the parents not to worry." Eventually, however, experts left and right would link family disintegration to jumps in crime, anger, depression, and social dysfunction, with one analyst lamenting the new "moral wilderness filled with children seeking revenge against older generations who have seemed to turn their back on them."

The sixties ended messily. America sustained a series of unprecedented blows in the decade leading up to the 1980 election. So many aspects of the Vietnam debacle would haunt America: the loss of life; the loss of credibility among generals, politicians, and parents; the loss of a foreign policy consensus; and, eventually, the loss of Vietnam itself. As the United States retreated from Vietnam, it endured the oil embargo and the Watergate crisis, culminating in a runaway inflation, and the first presidential resignation. Gerald Ford's tenure suffered from his unpopular Nixon pardon, South Vietnam's collapse, and clashes about busing, even in the supposedly enlightened North. Pillars of the society, from New York City to Chrysler, flirted with bankruptcy. A host of either-or polarizing issues emerged that resisted the American instinct for compromise. There seemed to be no middle ground on abortion, drug use, busing, or women's liberation. When Americans celebrated their nation's bicentennial in 1976, the country was reeling.

The political, economic, diplomatic, military, and social hits were bad enough, but Americans seemed strangely unable to cope with these challenges. Americans appeared resigned and fed up. Their faith in their government ebbed, as did their faith in their own effectiveness. In 1959, 85 percent of Americans surveyed considered their "political institutions" the source of their greatest pride in their country. By 1973, 66 percent polled were "dissatisfied" with the government. At the same time, the percent of people who believed that what they thought "doesn't count much anymore" jumped from 37 percent in 1966 to 61 percent in 1973. Clint Eastwood's *Dirty Harry* and other Hollywood movies caricatured mayors, police chiefs, and bosses of any kind as sniveling, bureaucratic, and ineffectual. Many responded by abandoning the public sphere, following, as the former yippie Jerry Rubin did, a "journey into myself." Others stewed. The bicentennial-year hit movie *Network* had Americans shouting out their windows: "I'M MAD AS HELL AND I'M NOT GOING TO TAKE IT ANYMORE."

Americans' new combination of resignation and anger threatened the body politic. "This is the great danger America faces," Congresswoman

Barbara Jordan warned at the 1976 Democratic convention, "that we will cease to be one nation and become instead a collection of interest groups; city against suburb, region against region, individual against individual. Each seeking to satisfy private wants." By 1980 a new phrase, NIMBY, represented citizens' response to proposals to build landfills, prisons, sometimes even schools or factories near their homes: "Not in My Back Yard."

The energy-inflation dynamic illustrated how America's psychic crisis exacerbated substantive challenges. Thanks to the Arab oil embargo, crude oil prices tripled from the fall of 1973 to New Year's Day, 1974. As the gas-pump prices soared from thirty cents to over a dollar per gallon, inflation mushroomed. Wholesale prices jumped 14 percent from 1973 to 1974, making a 1967 dollar in consumer prices worth sixty-eight cents. The age of the great inflation had arrived.

Surprisingly, Japan, an energy-addicted island with far fewer natural resources than the United States, did not suffer the same inflation. The oil shock that hit the United States created ripple effects due to structural economic weaknesses and the crisis of confidence. The economy took longer to recover as Americans struggled with a new curse, stagflation, a one-two punch of unemployment soaring along with inflation.

This same downward spiral overwhelmed many American cities. Fear, frustration, and defeatism exacerbated urban economic and social problems, especially in the northern Rust Belt. As factories closed and America lurched from a manufacturing economy to a service economy, *Business Week* questioned America's "economic viability." From 1969 to 1979, industries representing seventeen thousand jobs a year left Cleveland, part of an estimated loss that decade of thirty-two to thirty-eight million American jobs due to what analysts called the "deindustrialization of America." With steel, chemical, and auto part plants closing, with old houses collapsing, with the infrastructure of streets, sewers, bridges, and tunnels crumbling, with the urban budget tanking, with schools deteriorating, and with crime and taxation rising, middle- and upper-middle-class whites began fleeing to the suburbs, and to the Sun Belt. Cleveland lost 9.6 percent of its population from 1970 to 1973. By 1980 the population of 572,532 was back to 1910 levels.

Along with other cities such as St. Louis, Detroit, Philadelphia, and Baltimore, Cleveland relied on federal grants for over half its revenues. Mismanagement and turf battles compounded the problem. Cleveland defaulted on fourteen million dollars in notes to local banks, the first big city to default since the Depression. The populist antics of Dennis Kucinich, the thirty-two-year-old "boy mayor," infuriated civic leaders and invited coast-to-coast mockery. "Welcome to the banana republic of Cleveland," one businessman sighed.

The failures resonated in city halls, state houses, and the White House. By the 1960s the American presidency had become the keystone of American political culture. It now became the focal point of America's rush toward disaster. A litany of aborted presidencies began with John F. Kennedy's assassination in 1963, Lyndon B. Johnson's premature retirement in 1969, Richard Nixon's forced resignation in 1974, and Gerald Ford's embarrassing defeat in 1976. "We've been a nation adrift for too long," Jimmy Carter preached in 1976. "We want to have faith again! We want to be proud again!"

Unfortunately, Carter soon joined this march of failure. Carter squandered goodwill with his arrogance, amateurism, impulsiveness, and half-measures. He seemed unable to whip inflation, manage the energy crisis, tame the media, or master foreign affairs. He alienated liberals by cutting the budget and deregulating the airlines, trucking, and banking; he shocked conservatives by embracing new values, boosting the minimum wage, and chiding cold war allies for human rights violations. By June 1979 Carter was less popular than either Johnson or Ford at their respective nadirs, with a record low of 33 percent approval. Increasingly, and characteristically for the times, experts were beginning to question the viability of American democracy and the presidency.

The year preceding Carter's reelection effort was particularly horrible. On November 4, 1979, Iranian "students" overran the U.S. Embassy in Teheran and took over fifty Americans hostage. The daily count on the news—"America held hostage," "Day 112"—epitomized American impotence, as did ABC's new 11:30 P.M. "Iran reports," often hosted by a journeyman reporter Ted Koppel, which in March 1980 became a regular news program, *Nightline*. Six weeks after the hostage-taking—two days after Christmas—the Soviets began a massive airlift into Afghanistan that would eventually land nearly eighty thousand troops there. Carter, who had hoped to befriend the Soviet Union, felt betrayed. That spring, a rescue attempt to free the hostages failed, with America's commando units defeated by mechanical failure and desert sandstorms. Eight soldiers died. The Carter administration, according to Henry Kissinger in 1980, "has managed the extraordinary feat of having, at one and the same time, the worst relations with our allies, the worst relations with our adversaries, and the most serious upheavals in the developing world since the end of the Second World War."

These foreign policy challenges occurred amid domestic mayhem. Senator Edward Kennedy challenged Carter for the Democratic nomination. By July, although Kennedy lost, Carter had to alternate preparing his convention acceptance speech with slogging through personal records to refute allegations about improper contacts between his brother Billy and the Libyan government. And as the countdown to November 1980 began, mortgage rates hit 20 percent and inflation hit 13.3 percent for 1979, and another 12.4 percent in 1980. Economic growth, which had averaged 2.2 per year from 1948 to 1973, limped in at 1.2 percent per year for 1980. Carter would title the chapter of his memoirs covering that summer "Beleaguered."

## Seeking the Right—and Left—Answers

While Americans—and their president—suffered, they also searched for solutions. From the left, many hoped to complete the 1960s' unfinished business. On the right, many hoped to turn back the clock and exorcise the spirit of the sixties.

It is too facile to conclude that in the 1970s the movements from the sixties flagged. While the civil rights movement, the sexual revolution, and feminism seemed to lose momentum, each progressed. Richard Nixon, despite being the Left's bête noire, institutionalized many Great Society reforms. Social spending under Nixon went from $55 billion, constituting 28 percent of the budget, to $132 billion or 40 percent of the budget. The Federal Register listing governmental regulations grew 19 percent under Johnson, 121 percent under Nixon, and 27 percent under Carter, weighing in at 87,102 pages by 1980. Nixon also presided over the government at a time when many of the movement's initiatives became standard operating procedures. The story of liberalism in the 1970s, therefore, is more than fights over affirmative action, abortion, busing, and the equal rights amendment. In the 1970s these movements consolidated their hold on American politics and culture. From a gun-shy diplomacy to a healthy skepticism about the government line, the movement sensibility—and critique— endured.

In the 1970s there was a great deflection from politics to culture, from statecraft to lifestyle. The focus of the battle shifted from the streets and the corridors of power to the homes and the schools. The sixties' look—which had been the province of a relatively small elite— went mainstream in the 1970s. Jeans and granola, long hair and marijuana spread from college to high school, from elite enclaves to Main Street U.S.A. Living and looking like a hippie was no longer the statement it had been as the behavior and the look became ubiquitous.

The women's movement would emerge as perhaps the most influential movement of the 1960s, and in the 1970s it made major strides. In 1970 only 30 percent of women with children under six worked; by 1985 more than half did. Women rushed into the professions, transforming their work environments, their families, and the society, along with their own destinies. By 1984 one-third of law graduates were female, up from 3.6 percent in 1962 and 12 percent in 1972. By 1978 more women than men were entering college, revolutionizing the way Americans learned and earned, lived and loved.

The spread of these movements also provoked some backlash movements, from grassroots tax rebels to the Christian fundamentalists' "Moral Majority." In 1964 pundits declared that President Lyndon Johnson's landslide victory over Arizona Senator Barry Goldwater buried American conservatism for a generation. Actually, Goldwater's unapologetic right-wing crusade helped reorient the movement ideologically and tactically. Twenty-seven million people voted for Goldwater—a total dwarfed by the 43 million who voted for Johnson, but one similar to the 31 million who would vote for the liberal Hubert Humphrey in 1968, and the 29 million who would vote for George

McGovern's 1972 antiwar campaign. Moreover, an impressive 3.9 million Americans worked for Goldwater, providing a dynamic nucleus for the future. The Goldwater campaign also marked the national political debut of the Moses who would eventually lead the conservatives out of their wilderness, Ronald Reagan.

To win in American politics, conservatives had to stop being so grouchy. Conservatives kept long lists of people they despised, programs they hated, innovations they feared, movements they abhorred. Caught by their instinctive disdain for the liberals' instinctive faith in finding the right government program for every problem, conservatives flirted with policy nihilism; their clear sense of what they did not want preempted discussion of what they did want. After Goldwater's defeat, the new House minority leader Gerald Ford struggled to counter the "widespread, but erroneous, impression that Republicans have no constructive ideas." Liberals were too quick to invent new agencies to try to eliminate enduring human miseries; conservatives were too likely to mutter "Let them eat cake." "Whether the problem is crime or woefully inadequate educational systems we must present well-rounded, thoughtful, complete, precise, specific, responsible, compassionate and philosophically sound solutions," Congressman Mickey Edwards, a committed conservative, insisted in 1978. "To tell an elderly widow she must die of exposure because she cannot pay her utility bills, or to tell her she must eat dog food because the Constitution ordains promotion, not provision, of the public welfare, is incorrect and absurd. . . . Opposition to wrong solutions is not a political program."

## Ronald Reagan's Goldwater-Conservatism-with-a-Smile

The 1964 election taught that conservatism needed a lighter touch and pragmatic leadership. Lyndon Johnson's Democrats caricatured Goldwater and his people as cranky, trigger-happy Neanderthals, defying the era's progressive optimism. The conservative movement was so weak that American historians had bleached conservatism from the American tradition, transforming Thomas Jefferson's inaugural hope, "We are all Republicans, we are all Federalists," into the Louis Hartz and Richard Hofstadter consensus dictum that we are all liberals. In fact, the sixties' supposed liberal utopia would resurrect American conservatism. While liberal fireworks on campus monopolized attention, conservatives quietly stoked ideological flames that would prove more combustible and enduring. Reagan could motivate Americans by identifying many challenges that infuriated them, while reassuring them that they would overcome. "We have a rendezvous with destiny," Reagan proclaimed in what became known as "The Speech," broadcast on NBC on October 27, 1964. "We'll preserve for our children this, the last best hope of man on earth, or we'll sentence them to take the last step into a thousand years of darkness."

This tension, the fear of plunging into interminable "darkness" balanced by faith in American "hope," resonated throughout Reagan's life. Born in 1911, the son of an alcoholic shoe salesman, spending much of his unsettled boyhood in the all-American town of Dixon, Illinois, Reagan used his sunny personality to obscure his anxiety that neighbors would discover his father's secret. Young Reagan even adjusted his own name to improve his image, calling himself "Dutch" because "Ronald" was not "rugged enough for a young red blooded-American boy." As a part of the Hollywood dream factory of the 1930s, 1940s, and 1950s, Reagan starred in films that entertained Americans by upsetting them, then delivering the requisite happy ending. To survive in Hollywood, Reagan had to project the necessary self-confidence to win the next role while struggling with the actor's insecurity that every completed job was his last one. At home, as a member of what Warner Brothers called "one of the most important First Families of the film colony," Reagan played the role of the happy husband, the "Mr. Norm" the fan magazines demanded, while covering up the strains that ultimately destroyed his first marriage to Jane Wyman. "I *was* divorced in the sense that the decision was made by someone else," Reagan would say, demonstrating characteristic passivity in the face of crisis.

In the 1950s, while in his forties, Reagan rebuilt his life. He remarried—an actress, Nancy Davis. He started a new family, with daughter Patti born just seven months after the Reagans' 1952 marriage, and Ronald Prescott Reagan born six years later, joining Maureen and

Michael, the two children from his first marriage. And he transitioned toward a new career, getting a second wind in Hollywood by hosting television's *General Electric Theater,* and traversing the country as GE's "Ambassador of the Film World." As the actor evolved into the politician, Reagan continued his balancing act. Reagan's opponent in the 1966 California gubernatorial campaign, the incumbent Democrat Pat Brown, treated Reagan as if he were Goldwater. "Like Barry Goldwater, he is the spokesman for a harsh philosophy of doom and darkness," Brown snapped. But it was hard to pin that tag on such a charming optimist. Goldwater was likely to sneer, as he had in 1962, that the University of Colorado was "a haven for un-American ideas"; Reagan, by contrast, laughed that student radicals "act like Tarzan, look like Jane, and smell like Cheetah." Similarly, at his swearing-in ceremony as governor—having dispatched Brown handily—Reagan addressed his fellow citizens and movement allies, saying, "For many years now, you and I have been shushed like children and told there are no simple answers to complex problems which are beyond our comprehension. Well, the truth is, there are simple answers—but there are no easy ones."

Even critics marveled at Reagan's finesse, his ease in his own skin, his comfort at the helm. "The former California governor is a bright, if not original, thinker. He radiates traditional American values," the editor of the leftist *Nation,* Carey McWilliams, wrote in June 1980. "He is not a hater. He likes people. He appears to feel that there is good in almost everyone. He is a very secure man; what you see is what he is."

In a dynamic all-too-familiar to many couples, Nancy Reagan's more brittle mien accentuated Ronald Reagan's reputation for niceness. Mrs. Reagan's 1950s-style protective ways and adoring gaze enraged feminists and many of the female journalists covering her. "Nancy, people just don't *believe* it when you look at Ronnie that way— as though you're saying, 'He's my hero,'" a friend warned. Mrs. Reagan responded, "but he *is* my hero."

The resulting cultural and political crossfire helped cast the Reagans as role models for America's embattled traditionalists. Blinded by their hostility, critics would deploy many sexist clichés to mock the woman Ronald Reagan called "Mommy." Nancy Reagan became the heavy, the "Lady Macbeth" who lured the once-Democratic union leader toward the dark side of conservatism, the striver who pushed him into politics, the "Dragon Lady" who terrified the help. Contrasting the genial husband and stressed-out wife, such stereotypes helped maintain that sunny aura that served Reagan so well.

Reagan's Goldwater-conservatism-with-a-smile would unite disparate constituencies: Protestant evangelicals infuriated by what they considered to be an immoral liberal minority's assault on American values; blue-collar Catholics frustrated that the Great Society did not help them as the New Deal had helped their parents; southerners estranged from the Democrats' civil rights agenda; neoconservative intellectuals alienated by the sixties' legacy and fearing Soviet expansion; corporate leaders dumbfounded by the Democratic addiction to big government and hostility to big business; homeowners crushed by the double whammy of an eroding dollar and soaring property taxes; and residents of the Sun Belt fed up with high taxes and burdensome regulations. The constituencies galvanized and mobilized in the 1960s and 1970s.

In many ways, the new conservatism was Reaganesque even before it was Reaganized. Maturing beyond the John Birchers' 1950s sourness, many mixed the modern gospel of consumerism with a reverence for tradition and a disdain for Communism. Speaking to everyday people in everyday language about everyday problems afflicting individuals, families, communities, schools, and churches, these "suburban warriors" shifted, the historian Lisa McGerr notes, "from tirades on socialism and Communism, and toward attacks on liberal 'permissiveness,' 'welfare chiselers,' 'criminality,' and 'big government.'" The resulting conservatism was more dynamic, optimistic, individualistic, modern, welcoming, expansive, popular, relevant, and American. Flashing the 1970s' smiley face, not the previous decades' scowls, this blow-dried conservatism was Marshall McLuhan cool, not Huey Long hot. It was a movement of managers and professionals, not farmers and union workers; of the car pool, not the pool hall; of the television studio, not the pep rally; of the Crystal Cathedral, not the Ku Klux Klan; of California dreaming, not Mississippi rancor; of air conditioning and deodorant, not hand-held fans and sweat-soaked shirts. More anti-abortion than anti-Communist, more Ronald McDonald than Joseph McCarthy, these new activists mounted tax revolts not racial attacks, seeking to improve their lifestyles, not save the world.

Gradually, conservatives relinquished the romance of losing but being right for the thrill—and responsibility—of winning but having to compromise. Gaining experience far from the klieg lights of Broadway, when their time came the conservatives took over the Republican Party smoothly, easily, having already learned from their mistakes, having mastered organizational and communication skills. In forging a party of the Sun Belt and the West, conservatives were not just fighting Democrats. Conservatives had to defeat the Upper East Side silk stocking Republican liberalism of Nelson Rockefeller and Jacob Javits, and the pragmatic Republicanism of Richard Nixon and Gerald Ford.

By 1980 the network of organizations and periodicals that sustained conservatives through the wilderness years had grown. Organizations such as the Young Americans for Freedom positioned alumni throughout Washington. Magazines such as the *National Review* were now integrated into the Beltway mainstream. Foot soldiers energized by evangelical churches and New Right direct mail appeals were primed. And while by no means hip, conservatives were affecting popular culture. *The Empire Strikes Back,* the sequel to the 1977 blockbuster, *Star Wars,* opened in May 1980. *Star Wars* "came out of my desire to make a modern fairy tale," George Lucas, himself no conservative, would note. "Fairy tales are how people learn about good and evil, about how to conduct themselves in society." Such myths offered welcome ballast in a society adrift.

Among highbrows, *Free to Choose,* Milton and Rose Friedman's bestselling book and popular PBS series, preached that "Economic freedom is an essential requisite for political freedom." While liberals would fret about "The Reagan Detour" in the march toward progress, conservatives would produce one provocative, best-selling, manifesto after another, be it George Gilder's *Wealth and Poverty,* Charles Murray's *Losing Ground,* or Allan Bloom's *The Closing of the American Mind.* These books spurred debate and changed the American ideological universe. Similarly, as the Heritage Foundation and the American Enterprise Institute began to find their voices, and their financial angels, these foundations and other think tanks would be to the next generation of conservatives what Harvard and Yale had been to New Deal and New Frontier liberals—both intellectual hothouse and meal ticket. Conservatives enjoyed an ideological renaissance. Budget-cutting talk spread in Congress as grassroots campaigns against property taxes in various states boosted the popularity of the Kemp-Roth 30 percent tax cut and faith in "supply-side economics."

Just as the American labor movement succeeded only by turning to "bread-and-butter" unionism rather than more radical, European, incarnations, the tax revolt helped create a successful, populist, bread-and-butter conservatism. Soft-pedaling their more radical views about the income tax being "un-American and illegal," activists such as the retired businessman Howard Jarvis addressed inflation-weary Americans' frustrations. They were tired of seeing their tax bills soar as their salaries grew but their earning power shriveled; they resented paying ever higher property taxes on a house they could not afford to leave, because everything else had become so expensive. In June 1978, when Californians by two to one passed Proposition 13, a state constitutional amendment limiting local property taxes to 1 percent of market value, it triggered what the *New York Times* called a "modern Boston Tea party" nationwide. Terrified, thirty-seven states would reduce property taxes, twenty-eight would cut income taxes, and even Massachusetts, known as "Taxachusetts," would face a referendum on the November 1980 ballot, capping local property taxes at 2.5 percent. Proposition 2½ would pass as spending caps also proliferated nationwide.

Since the 1950s, Ronald Reagan had been preaching against high taxes squelching Americans' desire to work. In his syndicated radio broadcast on the eve of the California vote, Reagan attacked Jimmy Carter's plan to make taxes more "progressive," meaning raising taxes for those earning $20,000 or more. Calling it, in his folksy way, "getting the most feathers possible from the fewest geese in order to minimize the quacking," Reagan asked "can we steepen the tax brackets any more than they are without being totally unfair to those who work & earn & make this country go?"

This was Reagan's gift. He could make what had sounded extreme in Goldwater's terms—and during Goldwater's times—seem reasonable.

"My definition of a Republican conservative is an American of integrity, progressive in his creative thinking, who strives to make this a better place in which to live and raise children, and accomplishes that result by the application of hard work and sound common sense," he said in 1966. "A conservative Republican is a good American citizen with both feet on the ground." As times changed, and his message resonated better, Reagan deployed ever more pointed anecdotes proving how illogical, voracious, and insensitive to the individual big government could be.

By 1980 the federal government was indeed a behemoth. The half-trillion-dollar-a-year federal budget ate up nearly one-quarter of America's gross national product. Spending on all levels of government consumed 36 percent of the GNP. The federal government employed more than one million people in non-defense-related services and doled out billions of dollars in subsidies to farmers, physicians, small businesses, oil companies, auto manufacturers, railroads, airports, exporters, and importers. There were dozens of federal agencies supervising, regulating, and micromanaging American life.

This greedy, growing leviathan, which devoured hard-working Americans' tax dollars, was also an angel of mercy feeding the hungry, housing the homeless, healing the sick—one of every two households in the United States received some form of federal, state, or local government support, 37 million individuals accepted Social Security assistance, 50 million children attended 170,000 schools, and a quarter billion Americans enjoyed the use of 29,500 post offices, 1 million bridges, and 4 million miles of roads.

Americans had begun to grumble about the bureaucratic regulations emanating from Washington, which cost private businesses an estimated $100 billion and generated ten billion pieces of paper annually. Many citizens, who on average worked mornings to pay the government and afternoons to feed their families, resented the arrogance of federal employees who could ruin livelihoods with the flick of their government-issued bics. Amid hyperinflation and steep interest rates, most Americans came to believe that the large federal budget deficits were ruining the economy. Still, most Americans expected the government to continue supporting the poor—and subsidizing whatever pet project proved useful in their own lives.

Nevertheless, conservatism's "happy warrior," populist pitch, and growing infrastructure could only do so much. Reagan and his supporters would boast of forging a cohesive conservative movement. In fact, this often unruly gang of groups alienated from the Great Society, the Democratic Party, and the Carter presidency found a temporary way station but not a home; a fleeting alliance, not an enduring coalition. Even as they tasted early successes such as the tax revolt, conservatives were discovering the age-old American lesson that ideological movements often achieved mass success only by betraying—or at least constricting—their beliefs. Congressman Mickey Edwards' 1978 lament haunted the decade: conservatives seemed unable "to consistently convert favorable public sentiment into legislative victories" or effectively "change or form public opinion."

## A Nasty Campaign

With morale plummeting and inflation soaring, with Americans and the presidency itself seemingly held hostage to the whims of Iranian extremists, with liberalism listing but still dominant, with conservatism ascendant but still marginalized, it would be a nasty campaign. Both candidates "are at the bottom of the list," one Virginian griped. "Carter is inept at making decisions. . . . Reagan is inept at thinking, period."

A rare ray of light appeared early in the campaign, when Illinois Congressman John Anderson boldly preached gun control to the National Rifle Association and peddled détente to the American Legion. Garry Trudeau, the cartoonist, was charmed, and the students who rallied around Anderson became known as "Doonesbury kids." Anderson's primary season popularity prompted an independent, third party run. This crusade would spawn a string of great white reportorial campaign hopes—independent, unconventional straight-shooters who enjoyed early surges. Reporters, liberals, and independents would swoon, the mavericks would flourish momentarily, before wilting under the exposure. Still, in a disaffected age, such lone crusaders as Anderson, Paul Tsongas in 1992, Bill Bradley and John McCain in 2000, and Howard Dean in 2004 would "inspire a generation of young people to get involved—often for the first time," one former "Doonesbury kid," Matt Gerson, would note.

If Anderson the straight-shooter was a novelty, Ronald Reagan was an anomaly. Reagan was a conservative crusader with a pragmatic gubernatorial record. He was an amiable ideologue, an accommodating extremist. He was charming but opinionated, glib but bookish in an anti-intellectual, *Reader's Digest* sort of way, rooted in the Right but wooing the center. The campaign contradictions would be the paradoxes of his presidency. "Let Reagan be Reagan," conservatives would plead during the second term. What they meant was let loose Reagan the right-winger. Yet in balancing, in contradicting, in roaring right while staying center, Reagan really was being Reagan.

Although Reagan was a crowd-pleaser, he wanted the job to advance his ideals. From the start he craved the presidency's bully pulpit. Explaining himself to a former General Electric PR man, Reagan wrote: "The voice from that podium is louder than any voice out there in the countryside." Noting Pope John Paul's recent trip to Poland, Reagan asked, "Would he have inspired so many if he were not Pope?"

Reagan wanted that voice to be conservative, and he did not shy away from that label. Having been a politician for nearly two decades, Reagan understood politics as the art of the possible: "If I found when I was governor that I could not get 100 percent of what I asked for, I took 80 percent." This kind of balancing, an approach honed during his years negotiating as the head of the Screen Actors' Guild, impressed the economist Milton Friedman, who said, "You want a principled man, which Reagan is. But he is not a rigidly principled man, which you don't want."

Reagan was a populist. This son of small-town Illinois had spent his life running away from the Midwest while glorifying it. But Reagan was happiest when occupying that Midwest in his mind, that nostalgia-soaked village where people were friendly, life was smooth, choices were clear, values were eternal, and the sunshine was golden. Reagan conjured that vision often and effectively, moving his party toward celebrating those honest Joes and Janes who were the legendary backbones of those mythical towns. Speaking at the Veterans of Foreign Wars Post 3181, in Florence, South Carolina, Reagan appealed to the broad middle road. "We Republicans have to show people we're not the party of big business and the country-club set," he said. "We're the party of Main Street, the small town, the city neighborhood; the shopkeeper, the farmer, the cop on the beat, the blue-collar and the white-collar worker."

Reagan's new populism did not play to the dispossessed, but to those with some possessions to lose. Rooted in post–New Deal prosperity, this was a populism of the new American middle class, of the post–World War II phenomenon that created history's first mass middle-class society. Building on the tax revolts of the 1970s, the silent majority's anxieties about the 1960s, and nostalgia for the 1950s, Reagan's populism resonated with millions who left the slums for the suburbs but still felt like "forgotten men"—and women.

Reagan took pride in his ability to play to Main Street, to marshal the statistics and anecdotes detailing governmental outrages he had amassed for decades mobilizing Americans against big government and world Communism. Years before Ross Perot blasted "gotcha" journalism, reporters debunked Reagan's tidbits. Reagan said the Occupational Safety and Health Administration had 144 regulations regarding climbing ladders; "Gotcha," it was 2. Reagan claimed General Motors used 23,300 workers to fill out government paperwork; "Gotcha," it was 5,000, mostly for tax (of course this figure could have sounded outrageous had it been presented first). Reagan also confused Indonesia with Indochina, Afghanistan with Pakistan.

Long-suffering aides often perpetuated the impression of a lazy, disengaged, even dumb candidate, rather than a preacher on a roll. Reagan was "stubborn" and would stop repeating something he had read "somewhere" only if they could disprove it. When reporters asked Guy Vander Jagt, the Republican Congressional Campaign Committee chairman, if he thought Reagan was shallow, the congressman replied: "It depends on how you define 'shallow.' "

Yet Reagan as populist preacher understood that, as one senior aide put it, "A campaign speech is a metaphor. You can never dot all the i's and cross all the t's." Reagan applied his "aw shucks" approach to the "Gotcha" game. "I've been on the mashed-potato circuit for a number of years," Reagan chuckled, "and I have learned from experience to be pretty sure of the documentation of a statistic or figure I use." In this culture clash with reporters, the populist commitment to the essential truth trumped the elitist obsession with individual facts. Mentioning the "mashed-potato circuit" evoked nostalgic feelings, while reinforcing his message that the details are not just unimportant but difficult to prove. The big picture counted, despite the quibbles of naysaying reporters and pedantic academics.

Such talk mollified supporters, but it unnerved many of the undecideds. Reagan came across as stupid or reckless or both. "He's a nitwit," one voter proclaimed. "I worry that Reagan puts his mouth in gear before his brain is running," one "undecided" told *Time*. "He's shallow, superficial, and frightening," said another.

More seriously, Reagan had not convinced many he could cut taxes and boost defense spending without breaking the budget. The "Laffer curve," named after the economist Arthur Laffer, claimed that cutting taxes could generate additional revenue by stimulating the economy. But the theory was unproved, and Democrats estimated the tax cuts would lead to a $282 billion revenue loss and budget deficits as high as $30 billion. Even corporate leaders were "lukewarm" on Reagan, a *Fortune* survey found, and skeptical of his "simple formulas."

While Reagan's economic policy risked ruining the economy, many feared his foreign policy could destroy the world. "We believe that a Ronald Reagan victory increases the chances for nuclear war," *The Nation* warned. One twenty-two-year-old nursing student admitted: "I'm afraid things are going to blow sky high."

Reagan did little to mollify those concerns. A reporter once asked if he wanted to "bring back the cold war." Reagan snapped: "How stupid can you be? When did it ever go away?" "The American people are not going to elect a seventy-year-old, right-wing, ex-movie actor to be president," Carter's right-hand man, Hamilton Jordan, sneered.

In an attack so pungent that some newspapers shifted it to the editorial page, Garry Trudeau's "Doonesbury" comic strips depicted a TV newsman's journey into Reagan's brain. The "reporter," Roland Hedley III, discovered an overactive "hypothalamus, the deep dark coils of human aggression," "many" frayed nerves in "the left hemisphere of Reagan's cerebrum, traditionally . . . the home of logic, analysis and critical thinking," and "The Fornix, Reagan's memory vault, storehouse of images of an idyllic America. With 5 cent Cokes, Burma Shave signs, and hard-working White people." In that spirit, President Carter claimed that a Reagan win would divide "blacks from whites, Jews from Christians, North from South, rural from urban."

Just like their California colleagues in 1966, Democrats in 1980 overestimated the impact Reagan's sloppiness and extremism had on voters, and thus underestimated him. Carter's statement backfired. Reagan seemed too nice to be that kind of demagogue. He had no George Wallace snarl. The attack diminished the president and triggered talk of his "mean streak." The backlash increased pressure on Carter to debate Reagan, setting up the Cleveland confrontation.

At the time, debating was a mark of desperation for both candidates. In the sixteen-years after the 1960 John Kennedy–Richard Nixon debates, candidates in the lead had refused to level the playing field by debating. In 1976 both Carter the outsider and Ford the nonelected incumbent felt compelled to debate. Four years later, Carter at first refused, and in September Anderson and Reagan debated. Finally, in the waning days of the campaign, Carter, now the defensive incumbent, succumbed and agreed to the one, ninety-minute, Cleveland clash before 80.6 million Americans on October 28.

In Cleveland Reagan's warm, blurry visual style triumphed over Carter's linear, formalistic, more print-oriented approach. As during the Nixon-Kennedy debate twenty years earlier, Carter may have won on points, but Reagan made the better visual impression. "I think appearance is more important than a whole bunch of facts—how you look, how you act, and how you present yourself," William E. Timmons, Reagan's deputy campaign manager, noted before the debates. To Democrats' surprise, Ronald Reagan, the lifeguard, sportscaster, movie actor, and Las Vegas pitchman who had co-starred with Bonzo the chimp, bested Jimmy Carter, the braniac nuclear engineer and incumbent president who had apprenticed with the legendary genius Admiral Hyman J. Rickover.

## Election Day Blues

On Tuesday, November 4, 1980, the weather was mostly sunny west of
the Mississippi Valley, but gloomy and cloudy in the Northeast. A satel-
lite photograph of the Northeast shrouded in clouds offered a meteo-
rological reflection of shifting American power dynamics. Americans
were particularly churlish that day, with their disappointment in the
candidates compounded by the unhappy coincidence that it was the
first anniversary of the Iranians' assault on the American Embassy.

High in the stratosphere, the *Voyager 1* space probe hurtled toward
Titan, Saturn's "mysterious moon," days away from its closest approach to the ringed planet. Alas, the technological prowess and idealism the *Voyager* represented guaranteed neither peace nor prosperity.
Gold was up, the dollar was down, and the stock market rallied hoping
for a Reagan victory, with the Dow ending at 937.20. Inflation continued its rampage. A new issue of Treasury bills with an average yield of
13.029 percent was the highest since April; corporate profits had declined broadly the previous quarter, although more moderately than
before.

That morning, newspaper readers would ponder some perennial
world conflicts, as Colombia contemplated another initiative to end its
rebel insurgency, the "troubles" between Catholics and Protestants in
Northern Ireland haunted the Irish by-elections, and Zimbabwe's dic-
tator Robert Mugabe threatened to seize white people's farms. In the
United States, the crime epidemic continued to ruin lives and fray the
social fabric. New Yorkers were "dressing down" to avoid attracting
criminals. "You can't walk on the street in New York and be female,"
one woman said. "I wonder if we shouldn't all wear chadors with our
jewelry and our bodies and our vulnerability underneath."

Election Day was a minor holiday, with schools and banks closed,
but it would not be the rollicking nineteenth-century festival with
torchlight parades, candidate serenades, and hours-long stump speeches.
Politics was no longer the national pastime. Politics now competed
with dozens of other diversions in America's leisure culture. In the
World Series, the era's two great third basemen, Mike Schmidt and
George Brett, had battled it out, with the Philadelphia Phillies beating

the Kansas City Royals for their first world championship ever. That fall, Americans laughed at the comedic chaos of *Airplane* and *The Blues Brothers,* cried at the pathos of *Ordinary People,* and sang out "Ce-le-brate good times . . . come on," with Kool & the Gang. Johnny Carson, the king of late night TV, kept Americans laughing by claiming to have consulted Amy Carter about "what she thought were the most important issues to make jokes about" and asking: "Who do you want running our nation for the next four years . . . Nancy or Amy?"

The best-seller lists also reflected American's colorful palette of diversions, as well as some common trends and fears. Sidney Sheldon's glitzy *Rage of Angels* introduced a female lawyer who bested two male rivals. Irving Wallace's cold war thriller *The Second Lady* had the Soviets replacing the president's wife with a double, while Larry Collins and Dominique Lapierre's *The Fifth Horseman* imagined a twenty-four-hour race to discover a thermonuclear device Libyan terrorists planted in New York. On the nonfiction lists, Douglas R. Casey's *Crisis Investing* "for the Greater Depression of the 1980s" reflected the financial anxiety; Richard Nelson Bolles' *What Color is Your Parachute?* furthered the quest for professional self-fulfillment; Douglas R. Hofstadter's *Godel Escher, Bach* offered post-1960s metaphysics; while the popularity of Herman Tarnower and Samm Sinclair-Baker's *Complete Scarsdale Medical Diet* fed the growing obsession with fitness, even as the trial of Jean S. Harris for murdering her lover, Dr. Tarnower, progressed through the courts.

The eighty-three million voters casting their ballots that day represented barely 50 percent of the electorate—only 71 percent were even registered to vote, with those who were white, middle-aged, and better educated disproportionately represented. Rather than swarming party headquarters for the vote count, most Americans would spend Election Night watching televised election returns anchored on CBS by Walter Cronkite, on NBC by John Chancellor, and on ABC by an experimental, integrated team of Frank Reynolds, Peter Jennings, Barbara Walters, and the first black anchor, Max Robinson.

The Cleveland debate proved decisive. Gallup polls estimated that Carter dropped 10 percentage points during the campaign's final forty-eight hours, one of the most dramatic shifts ever observed. A last-minute

Iranian announcement of terms for the hostages' release—timed to remind Americans of their frustration with Carter's impotence—combined with the Cleveland debate fallout to shift millions of "undecideds" to Reagan. The result came to be known as the Reagan "landslide," with Reagan winning 51 percent of the popular vote to Carter's 41 percent, and Reagan winning 489 electoral votes to Carter's 49. The Republican renegade John Anderson received no electoral votes and 7 percent of the popular vote, although 13 percent of those deciding in the last week voted for him.

At first glance this appeared to be an electoral earthquake, a "counter-revolution," as *Newsweek* called it, a "MASSIVE SHIFT . . . RIGHT," as *U.S. News & World Report* headlined. The Democrats also lost the Senate, losing liberal lions such as George McGovern, Frank Church, Birch Bayh, and John Culver. Democrats lost thirty-three seats in the House, including that of John Brademas, the House majority whip. They lost six of thirteen contested state houses and over two hundred seats from all the state legislatures. Pundits announced a realigning election, akin to Franklin Roosevelt's 1932 win.

Reagan bested Carter in the South and the West, solidifying Richard Nixon's new Sun Belt coalition. Reagan won over 40 percent of the union vote, as well as nearly half the Catholic vote, breathing life into a critical 1980s phenomenon, "the Reagan Democrat." Reagan wooed 24 percent of registered Democrats, an impressive figure that nearly constituted his victory margin. Carter's percentage of the Democratic vote plummeted from 81 percent in 1976 to an estimated 66 percent. Reagan, by contrast, received 80 percent of the Republican vote—a mark of party discipline that would be the key to Reagan's strength with the electorate and in Congress. Middle-aged white males made up the heart of Reagan's constituency, with 53 percent of men and only 38 percent of women voting for Reagan, while 57 percent of whites and only 14 percent of blacks voted for him.

Nevertheless, the landslide was less resounding than it appeared. The electorate's volatility offered one hint. The electorate's negativity was another. Peter Hart's polls found that "More voters held negative attitudes toward each Presidential candidate than in any campaign since polling began measuring such factors." The referendum was more anti-Carter than pro-Reagan.

The great conservative realignment was chimerical. Only 28 percent of those bothering to vote identified as "conservative," only 13 percent as strong Republicans. Reagan's conservative ideology motivated only one Reagan voter in ten. Americans had not turned conservative regarding welfare, abortion, or the equal rights amendment. Voters wanted lower taxes and fewer regulations, but they still considered government the national problem-solver.

Ronald Reagan, whom many still called "an aging movie star" rather than a former two-term California governor, had triumphed. In his campaign he rehearsed the themes of rebirth and reorientation he would cling to throughout the decade. Yet Reagan lacked the mandate for change most people thought he now had. Not only did Reagan lack a mandate, but with all the doubts about his extremism and his intellect unanswered he entered the White House as the most unpopular president-elect in modern American history. No victorious candidate since polling began in the 1930s had such a low public approval rating, had so many millions opposed to him. Characteristically elated and not intimidated, the president-elect set off to create a mandate—or an illusion of one—that the voters had refused to provide.

# 1981

# 1600 Pennsylvania Avenue

The Ronald Reagan Show, the New Dynasty,
and David Stockman's Reaganomics

I place myself in the "seller" category of leadership.
RONALD REAGAN TO MURRAY RATZLAFF, 1983

Ronald Reagan ambled into office amid a grand display of inaugural opulence. Not since the Kennedy debut twenty years before had an inauguration made such a cultural stir. And, as John Kennedy had, Ronald Reagan deputized Frank Sinatra to fete him in style. The legendary singer represented Reagan's Hollywood roots and the journey so many "Reagan Democrats" traveled from the New Deal to this new dynasty.

The president's thousand-dollar morning suit, the First Lady's $10,000 gown, the sixteen-million-dollar inaugural price tag, the private planes landing at National (soon to be Reagan) Airport, the limousines deployed on the ground, and the decision to mount the inauguration facing west all signified Reagan's new direction. The celebration of wealth reflected Reagan's conventionality as well as the anomaly that his odes to traditional values coexisted with his role as an avatar of American consumption, a maestro of materialism. While Reagan did not possess as big a stock portfolio as the moguls toasting his debut, he enjoyed another prized American asset—celebrity. Like his predecessor Dwight Eisenhower, Reagan loved socializing with wealthy men who had succeeded in one realm neither of these sons of the Midwest ever mastered. Reagan's inaugural revealed a characteristically open

American approach to wealth, not as something to be resented because aristocrats monopolized it, but as something accessible to be enjoyed, directly or indirectly, and worshiped.

Reagan would attract blame and praise for ushering in this new era of greed and ostentation. Yet an era often ushers in a presidency. Democratic politicians usually rise to power by riding a popular wave, not by convincing millions to vote for something radical. Presidents can shape the times, as Reagan did; they cannot create the times. The man and the moment were well matched.

The economic miseries of the 1970s undermined the legitimacy of the New Deal and the Great Society, just as the counterculture of the 1970s left many Americans yearning for the "good old days." Splashy consumption became a way to demonstrate confidence and take back the night. A week before Reagan's inauguration, one of Hollywood's legendary producers, Aaron Spelling, acknowledged this new opulent era by launching *Dynasty*, a prime-time television soap opera. *Dynasty* aped the other great prime-time soap opera *Dallas*, which debuted in April 1978 but only became television's top-rated show during the 1980 to 1981 season, when Americans seemed more concerned with "who shot J.R.," the scheming oil baron, than who would be the next president.

Ronald Reagan helped invent the 1980s in a matter of months. During his mythical "first hundred days," and in the months thereafter, the new president helped establish a new national tone, shaping otherwise inchoate stirrings. Proof of a collective desire for a new mood bubbled up in 1980. The national euphoria—and sense of vindication—that greeted the "Miracle on Ice," the American Olympic team's surprise hockey triumph over the Soviet Union in February 1980, demonstrated what the *Washington Post* called "hero-starved" Americans' yearning for a return to patriotism and national "self-esteem." John Lennon's murder in December 1980, during the presidential transition, underscored the sense that a new era—with a new ethos—was emerging. Lennon was eulogized as the ideological Beatle, the Beatle with the sixties' soul. By 1987 Nike used John Lennon and Paul McCartney's anthem, "Revolution," to sell sneakers, as public discussion of the legendary rock group centered around the modern gods of celebrity and money. Two months after the inauguration, Walter Cronkite would retire as the CBS News anchor. With his avuncular style, Reagan would replace "Uncle Walter" as the kindly paterfamilias of America's ever-changing family.

Like the B-movies he starred in, like the TV soap operas that would prove so popular during his tenure, Ronald Reagan was a man of standard formats, reassuring Americans by following scripts they loved. As Reagan prepared for his inauguration in January, the dynamic movie-making duo of the producer George Lucas and the director Steven Spielberg prepared for the June release of what would be one of the decade's biggest hits, *Raiders of the Lost Ark*. In this 1930s-style adventure, the screenwriter Lawrence Kasdan drew upon "all of our greatest, most productive myths about ourselves. Being strong, resourceful and quick. It's your best dream of heroism."

Reagan hoped to apply that optimism and heroism to save the American economy. While he was not quite Gordon Gekko in Oliver Stone's 1987 movie *Wall Street* proclaiming "greed is good," Ronald Reagan happily echoed his hero Calvin Coolidge that "the chief business of the American people is business." Reagan transformed Washington, DC, legitimizing a new conservative "counterestablishment," as Sidney Blumenthal would call it.

In 1981 Ronald Reagan was at the top of his game. The American people had not given him the mandate he sought, so he conjured up one. The 1980 election had provided him with only a Republican Senate, so he set out to woo the House of Representatives, despite its Democratic majority. Reagan swept into Washington, DC, with great flair. His inauguration promised to redeem the troubled capital city and the beleaguered nation, bringing the élan of *Dynasty* to dispirited Pennsylvania Avenue. His mastery of symbols was more than smoke and mirrors; in 1981 Reagan would focus on the meat and potatoes of the American economy and government. Reagan's young, zealous budget-slasher, David Stockman, epitomized the Reagan Revolution's great potential—and many promises—as hundreds of Reaganauts crossed the Beltway, moving into what antistatist conservatives had long deemed to be enemy territory.

By August of that remarkable year, Reagan had imposed a sweeping package of tax cuts, defense hikes, and government rollbacks on Washington's bureaucracy, and on America. His assertive leadership in economic matters and during crises such as the PATCO (Professional Air Traffic Controllers Organization) strike reaffirmed the presidency's potential power to skeptical Washington insiders, both Democrats and Republicans. Yet, never again would Reagan achieve such success. Some of these same dazzled, intimidated denizens would teach the outsider a thing or two about Washington gridlock—and high-stakes trench warfare. Stockman would see his stock plummet within that first year, as both savvy reporters and sharp-elbowed bureaucrats reminded the midwestern moralist about American government's "Madisonian," meaning fragmented, nature. This first year of the Reagan Revolution demonstrated just how far Ronald Reagan and his revolution could go, as well as suggesting how, and why, he reached his limits.

## The Reagan Narrative: Manufacturing the Mandate

After their November victory, Reagan and his men labored to hide one important fact—there was no Reagan mandate. A postelection strategy memo recognized that no Roosevelt-like realignment emerged because neither the new leader nor his program enjoyed mass support. The Reaganites would have to manufacture their mandate, and seize their moment, as John Kennedy had.

The mandate mantra was central to the Reaganites' success. Reagan's aides understood that mandates were constructs, "that political mandates generate both their form and force from expectations." "Reagan's mandate is 'change,'" they insisted. Literally underlining this notion in their blueprint for the first few weeks they wrote: *"the 1980 presidential election should be viewed as an axial event demarking a major political opportunity for redrafting the policy agenda."* Trying to "restructure the political agenda for the next two decades," they acted as if "The public has sanctioned the search for a new public philosophy to govern America."

The January 20 inauguration would allow Reagan to set the tone
and pitch his vision. Contrary to his reputation, Reagan planned the inauguration carefully. A White House report later stated—exaggerating
mildly not wildly—that both Reagan and his wife "were involved in
most of the details concerning the inauguration," opting for formal at-
tire and the ceremony on the Capitol's western side.

Meanwhile, an army of aides worked to conquer the behemoth that
Reagan had been denouncing for decades, the American government.
Even though Republicans had been in power only four years earlier,
this transition would be dramatic. Reagan's policy guru Martin Anderson helped assemble *The United States in the 1980s,* 868 pages of conservative ideas. Anderson would later note that "seventeen of the people
who contributed to or advised on the book held important positions in
the Reagan administration." Cabinet appointees would seize power
armed with the Heritage Foundation's 1,093-page guide, *Mandate for
Leadership: Policy Management in a Conservative Administration.* Old Nixon
and Ford hands collaborated with young ideologues to produce this
blueprint for bureaucratic revolution. As early as August 1980, a "pre-
election transition planning operation" had amassed a data bank of
30,000 prospects for 87 top administration positions and their 170 dep-
uties. Since the spring, a Policy Task Force had been meeting with 326
people divided into 25 working groups. These initiatives launched a
new, ideologically charged, and politically savvy generation into the
executive branch.

Talk of the Reagan mandate, the Reagan Revolution, the Reagan realignment reinforced the staff plotting. The year began with a valen-
tine to the president-elect, as *Time* designated Reagan "Man of the
Year." The seventy-year-old Reagan appeared as an American super-
man, a handsome, broad-shouldered "success story" who even defeated the aging process: "Reagan's face was ruddy, in bloom, growing
younger by the second."

The political analysis of this "boyish man . . . whose time had defi-
nitely come" was equally exuberant. *Time* deemed him "the idea of the
year," enjoying a "philosophical as well as personal" triumph. *Time* defined Reagan's "mandate" as "specific: to control inflation, to reduce

unnecessary governmental interference in private lives and in business, to reassert America's prominence in the world."

Tuesday, January 20, 1981, in Washington was unseasonably warm at 56 degrees. As the new day dawned, the two men who had fought for the privilege of being inaugurated that day followed their different destinies. Jimmy Carter, still president, was exhausted. His eyes bloodshot, his face unshaven, he had not been to bed since early Sunday morning. Carter was excruciatingly close to freeing the fifty-two hostages in Iran. The complex deal involved transferring to Algeria nearly eight billion dollars in frozen Iranian funds from twelve different banks.

A picture taken early that morning captures the surreal ending to Carter's presidential dream. A worn president sits on his Oval Office couch, massaging his graying temples. Wearing a casual sweater—reflecting recent fashion and decorum revolutions—he looks like a defeated college football coach. To his right, on the couch, sits an equally dejected Hamilton Jordan, Carter's chief of staff. Jordan's sideburns testify to his youth, and the trends of the 1970s, some of which helped propel him and his unlikely patron from the Georgia backwoods to power. In the corner, on a separate chair, sits an elegant if only slightly rumpled Lloyd Cutler, symbolizing the Democratic establishment about to lose its power. To his left, slumped in a chair, his tie loose, his left hand stifling a yawn, sits Vice President Walter Mondale, one of the 1960s' leading liberal lions. Mondale's pose says it all: liberalism is exhausted and defeated.

At 6:47 A.M. Treasury Secretary G. William Miller reports: "All the money is in the escrow account." President Carter graciously calls his successor "to give him the good news." But Reagan prefers "not to be disturbed." Three-quarters of an hour later, Carter's wife Rosalynn comes in with a razor, followed by a barber. "Jimmy, you have forgotten to shave and you need a haircut," she admonishes him gently. Three hours and ten minutes later, still waiting for the hostages to take off, Rosalynn returns: "Jimmy, the Reagans will be here in fifteen minutes. You will have to put on your morning clothes and greet them."

Reagan begins his day relaxed. While Carter has been enduring sleepless nights, micromanaging the Iranian deal, Reagan has been reveling in patriotic tunes and medaillons de veau, watching one hundred thousand out-of-town guests gobble three-and-a-half tons of jelly beans and consume millions of canapés. In a harbinger of the mass marketing of brand-name mementoes that would soon be drowning America in monogrammed junk, the inauguration was partly financed by sales of inaugural knick-knacks, presented in a sixteen-page catalogue. Guests snatched up $5 inaugural medals, $650 Boehm Nancy Reagan roses, and $1,875 bronze replicas of a Remington statue, along with designer scarves, ties, and tote bags emblazoned with Reagan's initials, RR.

Eschewing the Carter era's cardigans and jeans, the Reagans championed a new designer ethos. Americans wanted to return to glamour, evidenced by *Dynasty's* premiere the week before the Reagans'. Eighty million people a week would soon be watching this *Dallas* knockoff as popular culture echoed, intensified, and mass-produced these themes of the Reagan inaugural. Work on the show had begun over a year and a half earlier, preceding Reagan's election. "We sort of anticipated the Reagan era, viscerally," Esther Shapiro, one of the show's creators, would say in 1988. "We picked up on the glitz and glamour of it." Shapiro and her husband and partner Richard were baby boomers itching to upgrade. "I wore granny dresses in the 1960s. I baked bread, I marched in peace marches, I made speeches," Mrs. Shapiro said. By 1981, "I felt like dressing up again."

The Shapiros, along with the king of TV schlock Aaron Spelling, believed Americans had a "renewed need for romance." They set out to create "the ultimate American fantasy family," worth over two hundred million dollars and living in a forty-eight-room mansion. *Dynasty* would be a powerful cultural force throughout the decade. Former President and Mrs. Ford would appear in cameo roles, along with Henry Kissinger, mixing fantasy and reality. This yearning for glitz coincided with a new, fond "awareness of business," as the publishing tycoon Malcolm Forbes would note. "Capitalism is back in, people realize that getting rich is just somebody entrepreneuring."

Reagan's own conservative movement harbored an ascetic streak that recoiled at such excess. "When you've got to pay $2,000 for a limo for four days, $7 to park, and $2.50 to check your coat at a time when most people in the country can't hack it, that's ostentation," the conservative stalwart, Senator Barry Goldwater, grumbled. Radical Democrats such as Congressman Ronald Dellums agreed, blasting the "incongruity between President Reagan's apparent call for sacrifice . . . and the wall-to-wall furs and limos." Yet many establishment Democrats like Lyndon Johnson's aide Horace Busby acknowledged that Reagan had a mandate to bring a "class show" and suggested that critics were "hitting the wrong button to suggest that the U.S.A. is a dried-up, resentful little country." Leo Lerman of *Vogue* insisted that the poor also enjoyed the opulence. "People want to see well-being, which gives them a sense of security," Lerman argued. In Reagan's America, the glamour of supposedly "classy" displays would trump, or at least obscure, class resentments.

At 8:31 on inauguration morning, the president and the president-elect finally spoke. The hostages were in planes, awaiting takeoff. An hour later, the Reagans sat in George Washington's pew at St. John's Episcopal Church, and Nancy Reagan felt "history closing in on us." Carter and his aides now realized that the Iranians were procrastinating so that the hostages would not be freed "on his watch." "They clearly can't know the inauguration schedule," Jordan muttered, once again underestimating the Iranians, their hatred for America, and their special disdain for his boss.

The meeting of the incoming and outgoing presidential couples proceeded smoothly, if coolly, with the men taking one limousine down Pennsylvania Avenue, followed by their wives. Reagan later forgave the Carters, saying that having left the White House himself, he could understand their sadness. Never one to miss an opportunity for a democratic homily, Reagan said: "One of the great things about America is how smoothly we transfer presidential power." Recalling Rosalynn Carter's stony silence in the limousine, Nancy Reagan would sigh, less charitably, "Fortunately it's a short ride."

Ronald Reagan took the oath of office. The sun burst through the clouds as if on cue. Reagan's twenty-minute address defined the Reagan narrative and his mantra: "In this present crisis, government is not the solution to our problem. Government is the problem."

Transcending the contemporary chatter about "special interests," Reagan embraced "a special interest group that has been too long

neglected . . . 'We the people,' this breed called Americans." Central to
Reagan's patriotism was his optimism. "It is time for us to realize that
we are too great a nation to limit ourselves to small dreams. . . . Let us
renew . . . our faith and our hope."

Reagan's first minutes in office were his best. Striding into the President's Room of the Senate, Reagan signed an executive order freezing
federal civilian hiring. "This begins the process of restoring our economic strength and returning the nation to prosperity," he said. As the
inaugural luncheon in Statuary Hall ended, Reagan announced, "With
thanks to Almighty God, I have been given a tag line, the get-off line
everyone wants at the end of a toast or speech." The hostages "now
are free of Iran." Ayatollah Khomeini had given the old performer a
great gift to help "begin an era of national renewal."

After a shrewd courtesy visit to the Speaker of the House, Tip
O'Neill—who felt snubbed by Carter at the 1977 inauguration—
Reagan rode down Pennsylvania Avenue to his new home. He followed
the path of Thomas Jefferson, who, after his second inaugural in 1805,
rode back by horse to the White House, trailed by congressmen and
other Washingtonians. A century later, Theodore Roosevelt reflected
the nation's exuberance and his own egotism by presiding over a three-
and-a-half-hour inaugural parade of thirty-five thousand people. In
1976 Jimmy, Rosalynn, and Amy Carter walked down the avenue, to
repudiate the imperial presidency. Now, Reagan wanted to restore
American grandeur. A limousine whisked him to the White House reviewing stand. The hour-long inaugural parade would feature a sea of
American flags and eight thousand marchers, including the band from
Reagan's hometown high school in Dixon, Illinois.

The presidential parade route told a tale of America in 1981, illustrating challenges ahead and resources available. Known as the "Avenue of the Presidents" and "America's Main Street," Pennsylvania
Avenue grew with the nation. Named by Jefferson in 1791, the avenue
represented the separation of executive and legislative powers—and
their links. The avenue had been home to slave markets and music
halls, congressional boarding houses and grand hotels. It had wit-
nessed inaugural parades and funeral processions, the Union Army's

1865 victory parade and Coxey's 1894 "army" of the jobless, as well as the 1932 Bonus Marchers.

The avenue was striking, a grand canyon with mammoth government buildings jutting skyward, epitomizing the governmental gargantuanism Reagan detested. Yet by 1981, Pennsylvania Avenue had decayed. Depression bankruptcies in the 1930s, the government building boom of the 1940s, and the lure of suburbia during the 1950s precipitated the urban rot of the 1960s. During his inaugural parade, John Kennedy deemed the avenue a disgrace.

Although the 1968 riots after Martin Luther King, Jr.'s, assassination spared Pennsylvania Avenue, the neighborhood declined. Terrified shoppers avoided downtown, patronizing new suburban shopping malls. Kennedy's administration had begun to think about redeveloping Pennsylvania Avenue. As in so many other areas, Lyndon Johnson's Great Society implemented Kennedy's dream. As a result, Reagan paraded along a work in progress. Most encouraging were two projects finishing in the 1980s: the Willard Hotel's face-lift and the United States Post Office Building's $20 million renovation. Built between 1892 and 1899, distinguished by its 315-foot clock tower above its eight stories, the Romanesque structure escaped demolition thanks to preservationists. Since 1816 when Philadelphia purchased Independence Hall to save it, America's capitalist compulsion to develop had clashed with Americans' patriotic desire to preserve. "The Pavilion" at the old Post Office would become a model of 1980s-style gentrification, opening in 1983 as a "multiuse complex" with eight floors of federal offices over three floors of novelty shops and ethnic restaurants in a building graced with a sweeping atrium, flooded with sunlight from a skylight. In 1988, demonstrating again that being good to history could be great for business, Union Station would open after a $160 million renovation, featuring 130 "unique" shops, and attracting over twenty-five million visitors annually.

Alas, it was easier to revive one historic street or one decrepit railroad terminal than the blighted city. Reporters surveying vast stretches of the nation's capital described the urban "moonscape" of deserted buildings and burnt-out cars, peppered with ghetto litter—discarded needles, soda cans, and fast food wrappers. These were signs of what sociologists now called the "underclass," residents of these "inner-city war zones" who had succumbed to addiction, alcoholism, lethargy, and despair.

In these neglected neighborhoods, residents hoped for a change but feared rejection. Raymond B. Kemp, a local pastor said, "Maybe we're ready to say it's time to work on ourselves for a while. I'm not sure that's half bad. Maybe it's time to say the government isn't interested in giveaways but it is interested in helping people do bootstrapping things." Some of the overwhelmingly white conservatives who preached the gospel of people doing "bootstrapping things" were also moving into some of these neighborhoods. Most, however, settled in the city's white and wealthy Northwest quadrant, or nested in the suburbs. The focus that January day was on society's winners, not those left behind.

## The Debut of Ronald Reagan, Inc.

With Reagan's inauguration the conservative movement came of age—and came to power. Conservatives had constructed an alternative universe, a mirror image to the Harvard–Brookings–*New York Times* nexus few could access. Fueled by ideas, funded by corporate angels, a network of intellectuals and political activists inhabited an incestuous world of think-tanks and journals. The *National Review, Human Events, American Spectator, Commentary,* the *Public Interest,* the *National Interest,* and the all-important *Wall Street Journal* published and republished articles by scholars affiliated with conservative think-tanks such as the American Enterprise Institute, Stanford's Hoover Institution, Georgetown's Center for Strategic and International Studies, and the aggressive new kid on the block, the Heritage Foundation. Anticipating the age of mass emails, at the touch of a button Heritage could contact sixteen hundred scholars in its computer banks to advance an idea, or counterattack.

Reagan's inauguration shifted the conservative movement's center of gravity to Washington, DC. Once epitomizing all that conservatives abhorred, the city would increasingly be their home. Aping Roosevelt's

New Dealers and Kennedy's New Frontiersmen, these Reaganauts would establish roots in Washington, creating a "government in exile" when Democrats returned to power, as well as a powerful magnet luring Republican administrations rightward.

"What's important isn't Ronald Reagan," his first National Security Adviser Richard V. Allen said. "It's the set of attitudes he brings into office with him." Hundreds of "movement conservatives" embodying those attitudes populated the Reagan administration and radicalized the federal bureaucracy. These conservatives, in the words of Dr. Tevi Troy, in his book on White House intellectuals, would be "detail experts," insinuating Reagan's ideas into all levels of government. Terrel Bell, the secretary of education, recognized his inferior status, heading "a department sired by Jimmy Carter . . . and publicly designated for abolition." Bell resented the administration's samurai warriors, sporting Adam Smith "cuff links and neckties," self-appointed "keepers of the conservative dogma," who would mock Bell saying: "My, are you still here?" "Do you need help on moving expenses?"

The modern presidency Reagan inherited had grown too big for one man. Elections now offered Americans a choice between two opposing teams. In an age of weakened parties, the teams had a Republican or Democratic flavor, but the candidate dominated. Like a privately held corporation, the modern presidency ostensibly reflected the boss's desires, but the hundreds of appointees, managing thousands of workers, had wide discretion. In 1933 Franklin Roosevelt had fewer than 100 White House staffers, only 71 presidential appointees, and 50 different agencies reporting directly to him; half a century later there were more than 350 White House staffers, 600 presidential appointees, 1,700 employees in the Executive Office of the President, and approximately two million government workers. Even without a president as open to delegating and taking direction as Reagan, the inauguration marked a sweeping changing of the guard, the debut of Ronald Reagan, Inc.

More than just an ideologue, more than just a showman, Reagan was a politician. Through years in the public eye, and building on his own innate reserve, Reagan developed a certain amiable aura. He was no Lyndon Johnson plunging into a room and splaying out his insides all over in a manic compulsion to dominate and seduce everyone he met. Nor was he a Richard Nixon fighting his own retiring personality, hiding his contempt for most people he met. Rather, Reagan was ready with a quip, happy to gladhand, happier to have people gravitate to him, but not willing to "bond" too intensely.

As a politician acutely sensitive to people, Reagan understood that he needed to woo the locals, especially considering their hostility. His inauguration culminated a charm offensive that began after his election. As Nancy Reagan archly recalled, "Ronnie wanted" to show "the local power establishment . . . that despite our images in the Eastern media, the president-elect wasn't a shoot-'em-up cowboy, and his wife wasn't a fluffhead." Working the Washington parlor circuit, the Reagans even accepted a dinner invitation from the *Washington Post's* publisher Katharine Graham. If Graham was the high priestess of Washington's liberal establishment, her Georgetown mansion was the holy of holies. At the door, Reagan kissed Mrs. Graham warmly on both cheeks—prompting her maid to snap: "I hope she enjoyed that because that's the last time that will ever happen." But the Reagans would remain friendly with Graham and others—to the chagrin of many Republican revolutionaries. The head of the Conservative Caucus Howard Phillips thundered, "If by June the Washington establishment is happy with Ronald Reagan, then you should be unhappy with Ronald Reagan."

Conservatives would often be unhappy with Reagan's lighter touch, his pragmatic style, his compulsive amiability. But Reagan was more effective as a happy warrior than an angry ideologue. Reagan's hobnobbing also contrasted with Jimmy Carter's contempt for "permanent Washington." As veterans of Hollywood, another company town, the Reagans understood the game. Just as they always lived on the outskirts of Beverly Hills, they flirted with the Washington establishment without "going native."

On the night of January 20, the Reagans floated from one inaugural ball to another, eventually reaching all ten. As usual, to the thousands of overdressed supporters who had overpaid for tickets, the balls were crowded, chaotic, and uncomfortable. But to the envious television audience, it all looked glamorous. Typically, the warm, fuzzy image would obscure the messy realities, the big picture would triumph over pesky details.

Reagan's inauguration calcified and popularized the Reagan narrative. In 1987 Burton Yale Pines of the Heritage Foundation would detail the five key "lessons of Reaganomics": growth is good, the entrepreneur is a "hero," "fair government" is limited government because individuals "almost always can solve problems better than government can," "competition . . . breeds creativity," and all four together "create a dynamic economy." Reaganomics is "more than an economic theory," Pines preached, building on American "optimism," the "inherent dignity of man," and "the knowledge that frontiers are conquered by human energy and creativity. . . . Reaganomics is also a theory of how the world works and a theory of what man can do to change the world."

The forward-looking vision, rooted in an understanding of the American past, as well as the "inherent" qualities of both the American and "man" were themselves characteristic of Reaganism. Typically, here was a think-tank expert analyzing, validating, and propagating Reagan's ideas, which meshed with popular attitudes beyond the Beltway. For example, public confidence in business had grown throughout the 1970s even without the presidential seal of approval, rising from 48 percent in 1972 to 69 percent seven years later. Such a process typified the conservative echo chamber Reagan helped establish to spread Reaganism, and to build on the extraordinary but by no means inevitable success of his inauguration extravaganza. Strategists understood that "of all the demanding roles, functions, and titles a president carries, such as Commander in Chief, Leader of Party, Chief Executive Officer—the ones that will be most crucial in this initial period of Ronald Reagan's governance will be Teacher, Communicator, and Motivator." Thanks to his mastery of those public roles, Reagan now had his mandate to change as well as to govern. The coming months would test his mandate's reach.

## The Education of a Budget-cutting Wunderkind

With their sensitivity to the symbolic, Reagan's aides understood that "the central thrust of the presidency will be defined during the early period." Remembering the Bay of Pigs and other rookie fiascos, they also feared "making big mistakes." Reagan's team would monitor the first day, the first week, the first month, the first ninety days, and the first one hundred days—assessing the "symbolic as well as substantive values" of the president's actions at each plateau.

Reagan's White House ran, thanks to an impractical scheme that worked. Reagan relied on a triumvirate, deviating from the Nixon-Ford trend toward concentrating power in one powerful deputy. James A. Baker III became chief of staff. He would work closely but not happily with Michael Deaver, the deputy chief of staff, and Edwin Meese, III, the White House counselor. The patrician Baker, a George Bush buddy from Houston, represented the Republican establishment and the business community, providing the ballast and the bucks for Reagan's Revolution. The slick Deaver, a public relations wizard and Nancy Reagan's confidante, focused on the Reagans' personal needs and political image. And the rumpled Meese, who worked with Reagan as governor, was the ideologue whose conservatism would be tempered by Baker's corporate sensibilities and Deaver's spin control. The tension of three powerful personalities straining to go in three different directions somehow propped up the administration. The three created a team that was more moderate than conservatives wished, but conservative enough to terrify liberals.

The same was true of Reagan's cabinet. Conservatives distrusted the secretary of state, Alexander M. Haig, Jr., once Henry Kissinger's aide, and the moderate secretary of defense and establishment Republican, Caspar Weinberger. Frustrated, the conservative Senator Jesse Helms voted against Weinberger's confirmation. Instead of an ideologue as attorney general, Reagan chose a California crony, William French Smith. Treasury Secretary Donald T. Regan was from Wall Street—with no political pedigree—and Secretary of Health and Human Services Richard Schweiker was a liberal Republican, a dying breed by 1981. The secretary of education, Terrel Bell, another moderate who identified himself as the "only nonmillionaire," would deem his colleagues "the water gang," drinking constantly during meetings to keep the prostates functioning, for "ours was not a youthful group." The columnist Patrick Buchanan acknowledged the cabinet's "competence" but asked: "Where is the dash, color and controversy—the customary concomitants of a Reagan campaign?" The only fire-and-brimstone conservative cabinet member was James Watt, an interior secretary hostile to environmentalists.

As the Reaganites marched into Washington and delivered marching orders to the nation, Democrats remained shell-shocked. "Each day's headlines arrive like war communiques," progressives mourned. "Strom Thurmond, who will now preside over the Senate Judiciary Committee, announces he wants a repeal of the 1965 Voting Rights Act. The prospective Secretary of the Department of Education has two children who have never spent a day in public schools. . . . There is talk of new bombers, new missiles, and old-style covert action."

Meanwhile, Reagan and his aides tackled America's "economic mess." On February 5 President Reagan's nationally televised address repudiated half-a-century's worth of domestic policy. Reagan advocated tax cuts of 10 percent per year over three years and budget cuts of forty to fifty million dollars in the coming fiscal year. The man most responsible for devising this sweeping "Program for Economic Recovery" was the new director of the Office of Management and Budget (OMB), David Stockman.

Within weeks of taking office, this once-obscure congressman had become the toast of the nation. *Newsweek* gushed about "the wunderkind of Washington," whose "frail good looks and boyish charms" complemented his "buzz-saw intellect." The *Washington Post* called him "the most important member of the board of directors the new president has assembled" and "a lightning rod to deflect the political outcry the policy will provoke." Even the crusty Democratic House Speaker, Tip O'Neill, marveled at Stockman's ability to tick off arcane budget items "boom, boom, boom. I've never seen anybody who knows the operation like this kid—he's something else, believe me."

Stockman truly was a "wonder boy." He had entered Congress barely four years earlier. This linchpin of the nation's economic program, this key to the success of the Reagan presidency, was only thirty-four years old.

David Stockman's story puts a human face on Ronald Reagan's Revolution. It illustrates a complex tale of taxing and spending, of employment training acts and aid to families with dependent children, of entitlements and block grants, of billion-dollar price tags and rosy economic scenarios. A midwestern farm boy who made it to Harvard and Washington, this baby boomer, like many, imbibed 1960s' radicalism before shaping 1980s' conservatism and materialism—by 1986 Stockman had become an investment banker.

Stockman was born in 1946 at the start of the baby boom, that transformative demographic tidal wave. Despite growing up as the eldest of five on the family farm in Scottsdale, Michigan, Stockman exhibited some of the traits of the stereotypical suburban boomer. He clashed with his authoritarian father, admired Martin Luther King, Jr., and rebelled in college, growing his hair long, marching with Students for a Democratic Society (SDS), sympathizing with the North Vietnamese. And, also typically, Stockman evaded the draft in a career-enhancing way, by enrolling in Harvard Divinity School. Ultimately, Stockman, like many of his peers, was too American, too soft, too bourgeois, too reasonable for serious revolution. These molly-coddled naifs preferred Peter, Paul, and Mary to Marx, Mao, and Che.

At Harvard, Stockman concluded that only capitalism could sustain the democratic spirit he relished as both radical and conservative. A brilliant networker, Stockman parlayed a baby-sitting job with the legendary professor Daniel Patrick Moynihan into a seminar entrée with the journalist David Broder, who recommended him to Illinois Congressman John Anderson. In 1976 Stockman won a congressional seat from a seven-term Republican, even though congressional staffers were not supposed to run against incumbents from the same party.

By now, the young congressman had embraced the free market gospel of F. A. Hayek and Milton Friedman. The Great Society's two-front war against Communism and poverty proved staggeringly expensive. Indexing Social Security benefits and other "entitlements" to the cost of living accelerated government obligations—and inflation—at a time of galloping inflation. Stockman, along with millions of others, soured on big government's social and political baggage, let alone its costs. By the late 1970s there were twenty times the number of amendments introduced per appropriations bill than there had been in 1963, reflecting growing congressional impotence and rancor.

In Congress, David Stockman found a soulmate—Congressman Jack Kemp. The ambitious, former Buffalo Bills quarterback converted the young congressman to "supply-side" economics. This fiscal gospel preached that high taxes and cumbersome regulations strangled the economy. Keynesian economics instructed governments to spend their way out of recessions, even if deficits resulted. More government programs would give citizens more money, triggering prosperity. Supply-siders preferred to cut taxes and manage the money supply. During recessions, if the Federal Reserve Board lowered interest rates, making money cheaper, more citizens would have more money, reawakening prosperity. Arthur Laffer, an economist, sketched his soon-to-be-famous curve on a napkin, illustrating that cutting taxes also stimulated the economy, and thus *increased* revenues.

"Supply side" repudiated the governmental status quo while promising ideological, social, and technological salvation to this romantic baby boomer. In fact, the social fabric could be restored if well-meaning government policies would no longer misguidedly perpetuate racism and poverty while breeding irresponsibility and crime. Stockman was inspired: "For the first time since my shaggy-haired days in the East Lansing coffee house, I began to feel as if I were part of a movement."

The supply-side siren helped revive American conservatism just as liberalism floundered. Yet conservatives remained in the desert, still searching for their Moses. Initially, Stockman dismissed Reagan as an "ancient" and "cranky obscurantist." The double whammy of 1980—inflation at 13 percent and interest rates soaring to 21 percent—radicalized Democrats and Republicans. The budget had to be balanced. The great end-of-century American standoff emerged. Liberals wanted to "balance up," raising taxes to fund the inflation-bloated expenditures. Conservatives like Stockman wanted the budget "balanced down," shrinking the unwieldy monster.

Stockman met another brainy young rebel, a former economics professor, Phil Gramm. On March 12, 1980, the Texas Democrat and the

Michigan Republican launched their "Bipartisan Coalition for Fiscal Responsibility," proposing thirty-eight billion dollars in cuts. A turning point in American politics, here was a rough draft of the Reagan budget, a year before Ronald Reagan's inauguration, with no input from California. By assuming the "appearance of being an expert," Stockman also had a dry run in trying to pass what would be the Reagan budget.

Stockman and Gramm helped reverse the national discourse: "For the first time since the New Deal, everyone was talking about cutting the budget instead of adding to it," Stockman later exulted. Between 1975 and 1979, twenty-eight state resolutions would call for a balanced budget amendment to the Constitution. Budget skirmishes began to monopolize Congress's time and reporters' attention.

Stockman recognized that "for better or worse, Reagan now *was* the voice of the revolution." Kemp insisted he had converted the former actor to the supply side. Stockman helped on the campaign, impersonating his old boss John Anderson during debate preparations, then lobbied to direct OMB. Still, Stockman never forgot his first impression of Reagan as "affable" yet "distracted," and with "only the foggiest idea of what supply side was all about." Stockman would keep the criticism to himself for years. When he finally let loose in his 1986 memoir, his portrait of Reagan was devastating.

## Finding the Limits of Stockman's and Reagan's Mandates

The myth of the Reagan mandate coalesced so quickly because Reaganite conservatism offered one coherent explanation to America's many problems. Reaganism blamed liberalism for the disorder and despair, the inflation and recession, for chaos in the cities and humiliation abroad. Reaganism promised to relieve the tax burden, repress inflation, reduce crime, revive prosperity, rejuvenate the cities, restore morality, rekindle pride, revamp the military—in short, to renew America. What Stockman and his band of theorists called supply-side economics, Reagan called common sense.

Throughout his eight years in office, Reagan would cling to his three goals of cutting taxes, eliminating regulations, and boosting defense.

The president was happy to see budget cuts, but he assumed they would follow if big government was sufficiently starved of tax revenues. Stockman's priority, by contrast, was cutting the budget. The OMB director realized that if Reagan lowered inflation, government revenues would drop—inflation triggered "bracket creep," whereby artificially higher salaries catapulted workers into higher tax brackets but lower purchasing power. The Laffer curve predicted that lower taxes would raise government revenues by feeding prosperity, but it never promised that the increase could compensate for the loss of inflation-fed governmental revenues. The Reagan-Stockman plan, like the Reagan-Stockman alliance, was doomed from the start.

Like Franklin Roosevelt, Reagan wanted to reshape the country in a "First Hundred Days" blitzkrieg. The economic crisis reinforced Reagan's political calculation that his illusory mandate gave him limited time. Stockman became the whirling dervish of budget cutting, chopping left and right. An equal opportunity slasher, Stockman targeted corporate freebies such as the Export-Import Bank, as well as the welfare state's signature programs. He wanted to cut defense while cutting education, energy, housing, and health. Only across-the-board cuts could tame the budgetary behemoth and retain credibility, he believed.

Stockman became the Reagan revolution's poster-child. Stockman's role was particularly important because the new president was not a detail man. "I place myself in the 'seller' category of leadership," Reagan would confess. Just as Franklin Roosevelt the master showman told two speechwriters fighting over contradictory policies to "weave the two together," Ronald Reagan settled arguments between his aides by smiling and saying, "Okay, you fellows work it out." Reagan's dependence on his staff suited the modern corporate presidency. In Hollywood Reagan learned that an actor was the public tip of a huge iceberg. One scene in *Knute Rockne: All American* involving only a farmer and a horse, he recalled, required seventy people on location. Yet Reagan had not made it to Washington without a backbone. "Some in the media delight in trying to portray me as being manipulated and led around by the nose," Reagan would fume. "I'm in charge and my people are helping to carry out the policies I set."

Stockman was crazed, enslaved to the difficult timetable the 1974 Congressional Budget Act imposed. The bill consolidated what was once thirteen easily padded appropriation bills into one comprehensive "reconciliation" process. The Carter administration had already presented a budget for the coming fiscal year, 1982. Reagan wanted to chip away at some allocations for fiscal year 1981 as well as for the future.

Reagan presented his Program for Economic Recovery to Congress and sixty million TV viewers during his first address to a joint session of Congress on February 18, 1981. In a thirty-five-minute speech, the president proposed eighty-three major program cuts totaling $41.4 billion for 1982 and tax cuts totaling $53.9 billion, averaging 10 percent a year for individuals over three years. He also asked the Congress to cut $4.4 billion in outlays for fiscal 1981. Ignoring the doubters who predicted budget deficits as high as $25 billion by 1984, Reagan estimated that his program would yield a $500 million surplus by 1984. Actually, the 1984 deficit would be $185.3 billion, and by 1988 the total U.S. federal debt would be $2.6 trillion.

The Reagan revolutionaries knew they were ambitious. The budget cuts were a means to an end. "With all the talks about cuts we can't forget that the purpose of our being here is to get control and change the direction of government," read the February 9 talking points Dana Rohrabacher prepared for Reagan. Even in this initial call, Reagan and Stockman acknowledged that they were proposing "a substantial reduction in the *growth* of federal expenditures" only. The program also called for tax cuts, regulatory rollbacks, and a new and more effective monetary policy.

Reagan tempered his conservatism with compassion, or at least the appearance thereof. Reagan's vow not to dismantle the "social safety net" illustrated America's consensus in favor of the social welfare state. Whereas David Stockman, the radical baby boomer, did not "think people are entitled to any services," Reagan, the Depression baby, did not dispute the government's responsibility to protect the "truly needy." Early in February Reagan safeguarded seven basic social programs serving eighty million people at an annual cost of $210 billion. Reagan limited his revolution by protecting Social Security's Old Age and Survivors Insurance; Medicare's health program for the elderly;

the Veterans Administration disabilities program; Supplemental Security Income for the blind, disabled, and elderly poor; school lunch and breakfasts for low-income children; Head Start preschool services; and the Summer Youth Jobs Program. With entitlement programs consuming approximately 60 percent of domestic federal expenditures, and with half of these programs subject to automatic Cost of Living Adjustments (COLAs), Reagan could only chip away at the budget with a toothpick rather than an ice pick.

And yet, even with these limits, Stockman encountered great resistance. He expected hostility from congressional Democrats, the "liberal media," and entrenched Washington bureaucrats. He was shocked, however, by his cabinet colleagues' antagonism as each one went native, protecting new bureaucratic turf.

Perhaps Stockman's biggest disappointment was Secretary of Defense Caspar Weinberger. Serving under Reagan in California and in Washington as one of Richard Nixon's domestic gurus, Weinberger became known as "Cap the Knife" for his budget-cutting zeal and bureaucratic savvy. Yet, now, as secretary of defense, "Cap the Glutton" was relentless, maneuvering to increase the defense budget by 10 percent per year, not the 5 percent Reagan initially proposed. When Stockman and Weinberger met with the president, Weinberger outfoxed Stockman by addressing the overall rationale for a defense increase, rather than quibbling over how much growth there should be. Weinberger illustrated his point with simplistic Pentagon flip charts, Stockman recalled. One showed a cartoon of three soldiers. The first, a pygmy with no rifle, represented Jimmy Carter's budget. The second, "a four-eyed wimp who looked like Woody Allen carrying a tiny rifle," represented the bespectacled Stockman's proposal. And the third, representing Weinberger's proposal, was "G.I. Joe himself," in full combat gear, brandishing an M-60 machine gun.

Stockman was flabbergasted. "It was so intellectually disreputable, so demeaning, that I could hardly bring myself to believe that a Harvard-educated cabinet officer could have brought this to the President of the United States," Stockman recalled. "Did he think the White House was on Sesame Street?"

Although not quite *Sesame Street,* it was time to play *Let's Make a Deal.* The fatherly Reagan said what he usually said to clashing advisers:

"Now why don't you fellas get together and see if you can work it out in this area in between." Ultimately, Stockman realized that to Reagan and his aides, "supply side" meant have your cake and eat it too. Stockman wanted to administer cod-liver oil—he proposed drastic budget cuts to fund the tax cuts and defense buildup. Stockman attributed his loneliness in the administration to Reagan's cluelessness and softheartedness. Stockman's revolution needed an "Iron Chancellor," not an amiable former actor.

## The Reagan Juggernaut Peaks

Surprisingly, most Democrats conceded a mandate to Reagan and Stockman. Alice Rivlin, a liberal economist heading the nonpartisan Congressional Budget Office, noted in April 1981 that the "public mind" now linked the problems of "the interfering government and the rising tax burden . . . (not surprisingly)." On Capitol Hill, many Democrats rode the popular wave. It was not just southern conservative "Boll Weevils," who had long been cooperating with the Republicans. Even Dan Rostenkowski of Chicago, the powerful chairman of the House Ways and Means Committee, caved. Looking back on the tax cut fight, Secretary of the Treasury Donald Regan would blame Rostenkowski for starting a bidding war with Republicans over who would give which tax goodies to which special interest.

Democrats were divided; Republicans, united. To Tip O'Neill, the true headline of the congressional year, and the secret to Reagan's success, was Republicans' remarkable unanimity on key votes. Inside the White House, senior staffers formed the Legislative Strategy Group to shepherd legislation. Chaired by Richard Darman, a mercurial, aggressive, and brilliant James Baker protégé, the LSG arm-twisted Republicans. When one, Iowa Senator Roger Jepsen, threatened to stray on a difficult foreign policy vote to sell the air force's sophisticated AWACS to Saudi Arabia, the LSG kept him in line. "We just beat his brains in," the White House political director Ed Rollins exulted publicly, if indiscreetly.

Administration officials were tougher with Democrats. In March Reagan's political operative Lyn Nofziger complained that some congressional Democrats had announced administration initiatives in their home districts. "Would you please tell all the Members of the Cabinet," Nofziger barked, "that god damn it, if they have any announcements from their departments that affect specific states or districts—they contact the Republicans and not the Democrats. . . . There is no reason in the world to give them any credit." Helping Democrats, Nofziger feared, might "damage the President's opportunity to change this country around."

The president was happy to woo members of congress with a softer touch. Reagan spent many nights calling legislators from both sides of the aisle, congratulating them on their birthdays, inquiring about their families, selling his program, and assessing where they stood. Reagan took his homework seriously, checking one after another off his list, and summarizing the call. "Mission accomplished. He sounds like he wants to help," "RR" scrawled after congratulating Democratic Senator David Boren on his fortieth birthday. "He's gung ho and working all out to bring about a win for Gramm-Latta," the budget reconciliation bill, Reagan reported after speaking to another conservative Democrat, Congressman D. Douglas Barnard, Jr., of Georgia. Reagan's congressional whiz, Max Friedersdorf, who identified many of the targets and prepared the briefing papers, noted: "A presidential phone call would do much to solidify the congressman's support of the administration on future votes." Despite being from Georgia, Barnard had "never received a phone call from Carter during his presidency."

In the arena of congressional relations that first year, Reagan's intelligence shined through, in the effective speeches he gave, in the subtle assessments he made of legislators' positions after calling them, and in the quick responses he filled out on sheets summarizing congressional correspondence. Regarding one complaint about "a lack of leadership" in the past on refugees, the president joshed, "but we don't have a lack of leadership now—or do we?" To requests to prevent a corporate takeover, he wondered, "more gov't intervention?" Asked about the Department of Education's "future status," he wrote, "I hope it has none." When Congressman Peter Peyser sent a poem opposing budget cuts, with the line "it needs understanding and a sense of fair play, if you give it all that, you will carry the day," Reagan insisted: "We're being fair!" In short, here was a president tackling many issues, sticking to his ideological guns, indulging, in the privacy of his study, in word play and repartee. Here was an engaged, supple, if doctrinaire mind at work.

Reagan's budget proposal provoked a power struggle between his Republican revolutionaries and Democratic defenders of the welfare state. Reagan's aggressive salesmanship and "'Godfather' tactics" outraged his rival Tip O'Neill. "Members of Congress have never been subjected to such White House pressure—not even during the years of Lyndon Johnson," O'Neill complained. Despite the momentum generated by his splashy inauguration, stirring speechmaking, and dramatic posturing, despite enjoying the first Republican majority in the Senate since 1954, the president faced formidable opposition. The House of Representatives remained solidly Democratic. "Every day we will be fifty-one votes short in the House to pass the President's legislation even if all Republicans vote with us," Vice President George Bush told the cabinet. The "permanent government" of Washington bureaucrats and media bigwigs remained hostile to Reagan's intentions. And while many Americans agreed that the welfare state was broken, few agreed on how to fix it.

Reagan's rhetorical assault on the New Deal triggered a cultural civil war. After feeling smothered for so long, the "silent majority" roared. White ethnics, nouveau riches businessmen, and America's petite bourgeoisie of white-gloved, church-going ladies with their country-club-joining Chamber of Commerce husbands lashed out against the skeptical academics, cynical reporters, sybaritic studio heads, and control-oriented bureaucrats who seemed to be propping up the welfare state. From the Democratic side of the aisle, Franklin Roosevelt's coalition of the forgotten, minorities, women, workers, and people of conscience mobilized against a mean-spirited politics of the rich. Among the top ten television shows, Reagan's America was the America of *Dallas,* the *Dukes of Hazzard,* and *Little House on the Prairie*—one of the president's favorites—an America of individual wealth, rich, colorful regional identities, and timeless values; "their" America was the America of *60 Minutes, Alice, The Jeffersons, Three's Company,* and *M\*A\*S\*H,* an America of doubters, aggressive minorities, single mothers, libertines of ambiguous but omnivorous sexual identity, and wise-cracking subversives.

The early skirmishes in this war soured the president's traditional honeymoon. Despite its Republican majority, the Senate Budget Committee skewered Stockman and other Reaganites. Prospects for passage in the House were bleaker. Reagan was running into trouble. The more specific he was about his plans, the less popular he became. Americans seemed more enamored with the idea of budget cuts, and with the budget cutter, than with the actual budget cuts. Furthermore, Reagan's activism—so essential to the success of his administration—risked depleting his already limited political capital.

By mid-March reporters declared the surprisingly brief "honeymoon" over. The president's approval rating of 59 percent was lower than most other modern presidents' rating two months into their administrations. "REAGAN DIP IN POLL TIED TO SPENDING CUTS," the *Los Angeles Times* proclaimed.

Reaganauts acknowledged the "resistance to change" and the ambitiousness of their vision but were undeterred. The president seemed unruffled. He was his usual affable self, charming legislators with his Irish wit, performing at his stage-managed public appearances, delivering the occasional speech. On March 30, as he left the Washington Hilton after addressing the AFL-CIO's National Conference of the Building and Construction Trades Department, the president heard "what sounded like two or three firecrackers." Jim Brady, Secret Service Agent Tim McCarthy, and policeman Tom Delahanty fell. Reagan and his bodyguards realized the president was hit only after they had sped away and Reagan had reprimanded his bodyguard Jerry Parr for such a violent push into the limousine. Once again, in a continuing and unwelcome tribute to the presidency's unique position in American life, a crazed lone gunman had shot his way into American history.

Few Americans knew how close their president came to dying. In mid-June Reagan would write to the widow of an old school chum in Eureka, "I'm very lucky and the Lord really had his hand on my shoulder. Literally, a sequence of minor miracles strung together to help me have a recovery that is complete." Reagan's "miracles" included the fact that "the entire surgical staff of George Washington Hospital were just concluding a meeting" when he walked in, and "I had the top medicos by my side in half a minute." Furthermore, "the bullet, which had glanced off the side of the car, hit a rib before entering the lung which helped stop it about one inch from my heart." And the bullet itself, a "devastator" bullet, failed to explode on impact.

Ronald Reagan not only defeated death that spring day, the old actor rose to the occasion, tossing off quips that obscured the severity of his wounds and mimicked the insouciant Hollywood heroes of the 1940s. When one nurse held his hand, he joshed "Does Nancy know about us?" He told his surgeon: "I hope you're a Republican"—prompting the classy response: "Today, Mr. President, we're all Republicans."

Americans delighted in their leader's sang-froid. Reagan's miraculous recovery offered a welcome bookend to Kennedy's traumatic murder. The failed assassination of the oldest man elected president helped exorcise the sixties' defeatist spirit, just as the murder of the youngest man elected president helped trigger a decade of national chaos and doubt.

The failed assassination had great political benefits. Reagan had already emerged as a man most Americans loved to like. His poll ratings shot up, a sense of patriotism soared, and opposition to his programs stilled, temporarily. By May 8, a little more than one hundred days after the inauguration, the Democratic-controlled House of Representatives passed Reagan's budget with a comfortable sixty-vote margin. "HOUSE PASSES DEEPEST BUDGET CUT IN HISTORY," the *Los Angeles Times* proclaimed, hailing the "270–154 vote" as "A BIG VICTORY FOR PRESIDENT." The first round of the Reagan Revolution reduced the personal income tax rate by almost one quarter and dropped the capital gains tax from 28 to 20 percent, yielding a historic tax reduction of $162 billion. By the summer, Reagan had eliminated $35 billion in domestic spending from Jimmy Carter's submission, and defense spending had ballooned. By 1986 the defense budget would be double 1980's allocation.

Ronald Reagan's public counterrevolution in 1981 was as dramatic as Franklin D. Roosevelt's "First Hundred Days" in 1933. That spring it promised to be as far-reaching as Lyndon B. Johnson's legislative burst of Great Society building in 1965. Reflecting the Washington tropism craning toward power regardless of principle, Reagan's swashbucklers